Launched in November 2014, **EPIC Television Channel** is India's leading factual entertainment platform. An India-centric content-driven destination, EPIC has redefined the infotainment genre by being the only native Hindi language medium in its league. The channel has been bestowed with several accolades, including the prestigious 12 PromaxBDA Award across various categories as well as the Indian Television Academy Award for the show 'Stories by Rabindranath Tagore'. Famed for its inaugural history and focus on mythology, EPIC has recently elevated its brand proposition and now showcases a wide array of original content across various genres. This critically acclaimed channel has expanded the scope of its offerings by including within its programming repertoire an eclectic mix of non-fiction content that aspires to imbibe the diversity of India.

EPIC has an extensive catalogue of original programming and a reputation for excellence in premium factual content that celebrates, explores, discovers and inspires India through untold stories, facts and possibilities—a channel which tells the story of the people, for the people and by the people of India.

Khwaabon Ka Safar

WITH

MAHESH BHATT

BASED ON THE POPULAR TELEVISION SHOW

Published by
Rupa Publications India Pvt. Ltd 2018
7/16, Ansari Road, Daryaganj
New Delhi 110002

Sales centres:
Allahabad Bengaluru Chennai
Hyderabad Jaipur Kathmandu
Kolkata Mumbai

Copyright © EPIC Television Networks Pvt. Ltd. 2018
All images courtesy © EPIC Television Networks Pvt. Ltd.
Transcreated by Chandni Mathur

This book is based on 'Khwaabon Ka Safar', a popular non-fiction narrative television show which narrates the stories of iconic film studios in Indian cinema industry. The views of the interviewees in this book are their own and based on their experience and knowledge. EPIC Television Networks Private Limited and the publishers do not validate or claim complete correctness of the views expressed herein. EPIC Television Networks Private Limited and the publishers do not intend to hurt, defame or criticize any person (living or dead), religion, race, emotion, religious belief, society, organization, institution, political party, etc., and their sentiments. EPIC Television Networks Private Limited and the publishers do not promote or endorse any such events or topics that may hurt sentiments.

While every effort has been made to trace copyright holders and obtain their permission, this has not been possible in all cases; any omissions brought to our attention will be remedied in future editions.

All rights reserved.
No part of this publication may be reproduced, transmitted, or stored in a retrieval system, in any form or by any means, electronic, mechanical, photocopying, recording or otherwise, without the prior permission of the publisher.

ISBN: 978-81-291-4863-6

First impression 2018

Printed at Thomson Press India Ltd., Faridabad

This book is sold subject to the condition that it shall not, by way of trade or otherwise, be lent, resold, hired out, or otherwise circulated, without the publisher's prior consent, in any form of binding or cover other than that in which it is published.

Contents

Prologue   *vii*

1. **PRABHAT FILM COMPANY**   1
   From Filmmaking to Film Institution

2. **NEW THEATRES STUDIO**   16
   Pioneers of Playback Singing in Hindi Cinema

3. **BOMBAY TALKIES LIMITED**   32
   Star Makers

4. **RAJKAMAL KALAMANDIR**   47
   Content over Celebrities

5. **FILMISTAN STUDIO**   64
   Cinema is for Entertainment

6. **MEHBOOB STUDIO**   81
   Cinema at its Grandest

7. **RAJSHRI PRODUCTIONS** 97
   Family Entertainer

8. **R.K. STUDIOS** 117
   First Independent Studio of Independent India

9. **NAVKETAN FILMS** 135
   Introducing the Urban Hero

10. **BIMAL ROY PRODUCTIONS** 153
    Where Art Meets Business

11. **GURU DUTT FILMS PVT. LTD.** 169
    From Cinema to Classics

12. **B.R. FILMS** 188
    Meaningful Commercial Cinema

13. **FILMALAYA STUDIO** 207
    House of Romantic Comedies

Prologue

Cinema is not just entertainment in India, it's a religion. With bated breath, every Friday we wait for the release of a new film. As for its commerce, the Indian film industry is the biggest in the world—producing more than a thousand feature films in about twenty-seven languages every year. Out of these, four hundred are made just in Hindi. Experts say that the Hindi film industry earned revenue of almost $4.5 billion in 2016. All these statistics make one curious to know how did the *khwaabon ka safar* (journey of dreams) of Hindi films begin?

Dadasaheb Phalke made India's first motion picture in 1930. It was the silent film—*Raja Harishchandra*, which successfully attracted Indians to the new medium. 'People were thrilled with cinema. Until then, there was only the theatre culture. There was Parsi theatre, Bengali theatre, and more such. But theatre viewership was limited to the upper classes. On the contrary, cinema was launched for the masses. It was sheer entertainment to watch the stories of kings and kingdoms, history, mythologies, etc. coming alive on a screen,' explains Ashok Rane, Director, Indian Film Academy.

Initially, Indian cinema was run by individuals. But gradually, film studios came up and changed the way the industry functioned. A studio was an organization and a place where artistes, technicians, finance, equipment, laboratory, sound studio and exhibition theatre were all present under one roof. It was a business model inspired from Hollywood. Ashok Rane says, 'A studio was where everything would be made at one place. The owner of the studio would be the producer. He would get money from somewhere and invest some of his own too. Everything—shooting, editing, lab work, pre-production, post-production—would be done at one place. From the peon to the director—everybody had their duty hours. Whether there was a film being shot or not, the staff would have to sit there as in any other job. There was a disciplined system.'

Prabhat Film Company, which was established in 1929, was the first Hindi film studio in India. It made twenty-five films in its fifteen-year-long journey, giving Hindi cinema many big names like V. Shantaram, Guru Dutt, Dev Anand and Durga Khote, among others. It was later made the Film and Television Institute of India (FTII), a premier film school in India, based in Pune. In 1931 came up B.N. Sircar's New Theatres, which made 165 films in just twenty-five years and brought with it the likes of K.L. Saigal and Bimal Roy. Then came Devika Rani and Himansu Rai's Bombay Talkies in 1935, which introduced the collaboration between Indian and German filmmakers. They made 102 films and introduced stars like Ashok Kumar, Dilip Kumar and Dev Anand into the Hindi film industry.

In 1942, after separating from Prabhat, V. Shantaram started his own studio Rajkamal Kalamandir—a studio which defied the star system, and focused more on drama, music and cinematography techniques. Another landmark studio that came around the same time was Mehboob Studio in 1943 where Mehboob Khan made *Mother India* and other socially relevant films. Rajshri Productions, founded by Tarachand Barjatya in 1947, offered traditional family entertainment, but also critically acclaimed films. In 1948, Raj Kapoor established his studio called R.K. Studios, which was the first independent proprietorship studio of Independent India. It mostly made romantic films that had subtle social themes. Dev Anand's Navketan Films, set up in 1950, was the first to venture into Hollywood's popular genre of romantic comedies. However, in 1953 came Bimal Roy Productions that made films focusing on social justice, great performances and melodious music, thus offering a cinema, which brought forth both art and business. Established in 1954, Guru Dutt Films made commercially successful as well as critically acclaimed films. Another studio which beautifully blended social issues and entertainment was B.R. Chopra's B.R. Films, which gave us the first multi-starrer Hindi film *Waqt*, and also the mega TV series during the 1980s—*Mahabharat*.

Amongst all these experimental studios, Shashadhar Mukerji set up Filmistan Studio in 1943, which changed the face of Hindi cinema with its escapist films. His studio made films purely for the purpose of entertainment—there were no other layers to it. It was Filmistan, which created the template for the well-known 'formula films' of today. In 1958, Mukerji set up yet another film studio called Filmalaya, which was mostly known for romantic comedies and for introducing style icons like Shammi Kapoor and Sadhana in Bollywood.

The show must go on, albeit in a new avatar. The studio system may have become a thing of past, but the studios stand tall even today and where films are still made to entertain us. This book brings forth the journey of these studios and their founders, who stood for what they believed in and pursued their *khwaabon ka safar* against all odds. These stories of personal travails and wins will inspire, create awe, intrigue and entertain readers, just as these studios' films did over the years.

1

PRABHAT FILM COMPANY

From Filmmaking to Film Institution

Founders: Vishnupant Damle, V. Shantaram, S. Fatelal, K. Dhaibar, Sitaram Kulkarni

Established in 1929 at Kolhapur, later moved to Pune.

Within 15 years (1929–44), it made 25 films.

The themes of their films were mythological, social and national issues.

They made the first Marathi talkie film.

The studio gave Hindi cinema many big names, like Guru Dutt, Dev Anand, Durga Khote.

This is where the unique filmmaking style of V. Shantaram was born.

Later made into the Film and Television Institute of India (FTII), Pune.

Maharashtra and Bengal are those states of India where there has been a long tradition of literature and performing arts. So, it was only natural for cinema also to establish its roots first in these two states. In 1929, Prabhat Studios was set up in Kolhapur, Maharashtra.

To put together the minor and major things of a mundane life, thread it into a story, and present it on the big screen is no less than an art. Prabhat Studio's films had the special touch of the Marathi culture, along with messages of nationalism and social improvement.

Established in Kolhapur, Maharashtra Film Company was a well-known film company founded by Baburao Painter in 1919, where V. Shantaram, Vishnupant G. Damle, S. Fatehlal and K.R. Dhaiber had worked together and learnt the art of filmmaking. 'These four had gained popularity for the series of successful films they had made for the company. However, things turned sour when Baburaoji began inviting film directors and art directors from outside of the company to make films and offered them higher salaries,' says Anil Damle, grandson of V.G. Damle. He continues, 'The four men had been with Maharashtra Film Co. from its very start, perhaps that's why Baburao's erratic behaviour led to enough dissatisfaction amongst them to leave the company and begin their own production house. On 1 June 1929, they founded Prabhat Film Company. It was financially supported by S. Kulkarni who became the fifth founding partner of the company.'

In the era of silent films, Prabhat Film Co. made six silent movies under the direction of V. Shantaram, the most memorable of which was *Udaykaal*. The censor board run by the British Government had strongly objected on the film's original title 'Swarajyache Toran' and so the name of the film had to be changed.

Ashok Rane, director of the Indian Film Academy, says, 'The makers thought that if the name was to be 'Swarajyache Toran', the term 'Swarajya' (self-rule) would be in it and connect it with the then ongoing Swarajya Freedom Movement, which caused a problem with the censor board. Ultimately, they had to change the name to *Udaykaal*.'

Prabhat Film Company was especially admired for one particular aspect: its production sets and designs. Damle and Fatehlal were ace artists. The talent that they had acquired while working under Baburao Painter could be seen in the first few films of Prabhat Films itself. They were a group of highly ambitious and talented people. For instance, the sets for their film *Chandrasena* were highly appreciated at the time.

The world's first talkie film released in America in 1927— *The Jazz Singer*. It got the ball rolling in several big Indian film studios as well, except for Prabhat Film Company. They still believed in silent films and did not join the race for the talkies. According to film historian Rekha Deshpande, 'V. Shantaram had thought of talkies to be a temporary fad which would fade soon enough. He also felt that it would take up too much investment with no guarantee of becoming a success. And why blame just Shantaram, even

Charlie Chaplin was of the same opinion when talkies began happening. Most people had reservations regarding it.'

In 1931, came India's first talkie film—*Alam Ara*. Sometime later, Madan Theatres of Kolkata released *Shirin Farhad*. The direction of the winds began to become more and more clear, and Prabhat Film Company, eventually, accepted this change. In 1932, came Prabhat studio's *Ayodhyecha Raja*, directed by V. Shantaram, which was the first Marathi talkie film.

Dadasaheb Phalke's *Raja Harishchandra* and Prabhat Film Co's *Ayodhyecha Raja* had a similar storyline, and by the time the latter released, the era of silent films was completely over. Govindrao Tembe was both the lead actor and the music director for *Ayodhyecha Raja*. He was fifty-five years old at the time and his heroine Durga Khote was just twenty-two. He sang in the film too—he had to sing on-set during the shooting of the film and the musicians played from outside the frame. This was way before the time of pre-recording. So, when Govindrao Tembe was asked to record his first song, he was asked to finish it within five minutes. But Tembe said it was not possible for him to do so, and that he cannot count the minutes and sing. He said he can only sing at his own pace.

So, Shantaram mimed the sound of 'one…two…three' while hopping behind the camera and Tembe was singing. It went on to 'five…ten…fifteen' and Tembe was still singing. Finally, the cameraman said 'Cut!' because the magazine had finished. Thus, that shot was cut.

'It was in that era that the practice of making films in more than one language began. *Ayodhyecha Raja* was made in Hindi under the name *Ayodhya Ka Raja* by Prabhat Film Co. and that kick-started the trend,' says Anil Damle. 'A Marathi film's audience would be restricted to Maharashtra only. But at the opportune time, V. Shantaram made the decision of making all his films in Hindi too. It was this very decision that made Prabhat Films a popular name nationwide.'

After the arrival of talkies, the next major focus was on music in films. And for this, Prabhat Films gave the local artistes a chance. Ashok Rane says, 'When cinema came to India, theatre was at its peak. So, its influence was so strong that when you watch the songs of these films you will feel as if you are watching a play in the theatre and not a film. Music continued to be that way until Master Krishnarao entered the scene and brought what we call film music in its true sense.'

Indian cinema was still in its nascent stage. Therefore, people were distrustful of the film business and those who worked in it weren't much respected. Educated, upper-class families did not allow their women to work in films. But Prabhat Films stood out differently, even here.

Ashok Rane explains, 'Durga Khote, who acted in *Ayodhyecha Raja*, used to live in Girgaon and belonged to an upper middle-class family. Her father was a solicitor. Watching plays was only a social habit. In Maharashtra of those days, to have knowledge about the theatre was considered prestigious. People belonging to the middle and upper-middle-class did not watch films, but only theatre. But just the way New Theatres became the pride of Kolkata, the same importance was given to Prabhat Film Company in Maharashtra. People of the middle-class would watch a film if it was made by Prabhat Films. So, when Durga Khote was approached for a film role, her family readily agreed because it was being made under the Prabhat banner.'

As the company began expanding, so did its needs. Thus, Prabhat was probably the only studio in the world which began in one city but concluded the rest of its journey in another. In 1933, Prabhat studios and its entire team left Kolhapur and moved to Pune.

'There was no electricity in Kolhapur. They were dependent on sunlight. Secondly, Mumbai was closer from Pune, which was important for the distribution of the films. Moreover, the raw stock and equipment which used to come from other countries were routed through Mumbai port. In terms of market too, Pune was more convenient. So, the founders made the decision to shift to Pune. They mortgaged a few things, collected some money and bought eleven acres of land with it,' says Rekha Deshpande.

In Pune, Prabhat Studio created such an enclosure for filmmaking that all the available modern conveniences were present. Individual departments were made in an organized way for various sections of filmmaking: sound, camera, editing, music, costumes; everything had designated individual spaces.

Anil Damle tells us that the studio of Prabhat Film

Company was considered the biggest studio in Asia, 'Keeping in mind all the facilities, they arranged everything like underground electrical lines. If a forest scene had to be shot then a little jungle would be made, ponds were shown. It's due to all this precision that Prabhat Studio was believed to be the best studio in Asia.'

In a journey of just four years, Prabhat Film Company had found its roots in the Indian film industry. Now it was time to soar to new heights. In 1933, Prabhat's golden period began with the film *Sairandhri*, directed by Shantaram in which, he tried a new experiment yet again. With rising success, rose the aspirations and the strength to do something new. *Sairandhri* was the first Indian film that was tried to make in colour. For this purpose, he had taken the film to Germany's UFA lab for processing.

Ashok Rane shares an anecdote with us, 'There was no colour lab in India at the time. Shantaram used to watch a lot of films; he had watched films of G.W. Pabst and Fritz Lang. He was attracted to colours. He went to Germany's UFA lab to get *Sairandhri* processed in colour, but it did not work. He did get the colour print back, but released the black and white one itself. Since the colour control could not happen on it, the film had become all red in hues.'

Failure is the stepping stone to success. *Sairandhri* could not become a colour film. But Shantaram's experience of going to Germany proved to be of value. During his stay there, he watched films by German directors and got very influenced by their techniques. The result of this was immediately seen in his next film, *Amrit Manthan* (1934).

It is said that when Shantaram went to Germany, he did a filmmaking course there in which he absorbed the German style of shooting a film. So, as soon as he came back to India he used a low camera angle to shoot *Amrit Manthan* a technique not used here until then. The low angle shots and circular trolley shots were used for the first time in India by V. Shantaram for *Amrit Manthan*. That had a major impact, the frame and composition enhanced the drama in the film.

Social reform has always been an active platform in India. From 15th and 16th century poet saints of the Bhakti movement in Maharashtra criticizing evils, like the caste system, through their poetries to Gandhiji in the early 20th century raising his voice against the same; social reform has always been present in the Indian society. The impact of it all could be seen in the films by Prabhat Studios.

Ashok Rane says, 'If we see the socio-political angle of India in the 30s, the freedom movement was extremely popular. The films that Prabhat Studios was making, they wanted it to have some contribution to the freedom movement. At the same time, Gandhiji was insisting on us becoming independent and for the citizens to work towards building a progressive society. So, Prabhat Film Company too wanted to do as much as possible for social reform through their films.'

With the release of *Dharmatma* in 1935, there came a major change in the music of Prabhat films. The impact of dramatization began withering away in Marathi film music. 'Master Krishnarao was composing the music for almost all their films. His style was a little different from his contemporaries, although the compositions were definitely based in classical Indian music. The change that Krishnarao brought was the usage of light music, which was easier for any ordinary person to listen and understand,' says Anil Damle.

Shantaram had, by then, become an established director and Damle and Fatehlal had taken the responsibility of all production designs and sound. However, in 1936, not Shantaram, but instead it was Damle and Fatehlal who had directed the film which broke all records of box office success in India until then. The film that ran continuously for fifty-seven weeks in a cinema hall in Mumbai—*Sant Tukaram*.

Sant Tukaram was India's first film that went to Venice Film Festival and it also earned an award there. Ashok Rane shares an interesting story from the Film Festival, 'Frank Capra, a then famous Hollywood film director, watched *Sant Tukaram* there. Neither was the film dubbed in English nor did it have any subtitles, he watched it in Marathi. Capra did not know the background the film was set in, nor did he know Tukaram or understand the songs. But he just watched the film in rapture. He was beyond surprise at India producing such a "wonderful film with such pure cinematic expressions".'

Sant Tukaram made 1936 a hugely successful year for Prabhat Film Company. In the same year came *Amar Jyoti*, made under the direction of V. Shantaram, which was an indication of the ideology behind Shantaram's upcoming films.

From the years 1937 to 1941, Shantaram made three socially themed films with Prabhat Film Company—these were very different from his previous films. Stories were based on social issues and told in an impressive way. The beginning of these films was with the Marathi film *Kunku*, the Hindi version of which was *Duniya Naa Maane*. Rekha Deshpande says, 'The heroine of *Kunku* was married off to an old man, but she refuses to accept the marriage. She rebels against it. The film's story was actually based on a Marathi novel *Na Patnari Goshta*, in which Meera, the protagonist, rebels against the social evil of a young girl getting married to an old man. She rebelled because she felt the practice was wrong and she did not want to be married to a man much older than her.'

There was a new experiment in the music of this film, Shantaram brought a new kind of realism to it. He used household items like utensils as musical instruments. Anil Damle tells us an interesting incident, 'The musicians went to the utensil merchants in Pune and asked for all the spherical water vessels (lota), filled those with water and tapped to check from which ones they could get the correct sound, and bought the vessels which produced the best notes.'

In 1935 came P.C. Barua's film *Devdas*, where the hero wastes his life in alcohol when he doesn't get his lady love. After the film's release, there was a race amongst the country's youth to become a Devdas. Shantaram was very upset with it. In 1939, he made *Manoos* and its Hindi version *Aadmi*, and criticized Devdas's defeatist thinking through it. 'It was his answer to *Devdas*. Just because you could not get that girl, why should you ruin your life over it? With that optimism he made *Manoos*. Its protagonist, Ganpatrao, falls in love with a prostitute, Maina. When he cannot get married to her because of the social taboos he too gets depressed and frustrated. But he doesn't throw his life, instead starts afresh. He does not get destructed with alcohol. Shantaram had made *Manoos* just to give that message,' says Ashok Rane.

In 1941, Prabhat Film Company made *Shejari* under Shantaram's direction and its Hindi version *Padosi*, on the theme of Hindu–Muslim unity. In the film, Shantaram made actor Gajanan Jagirdar play the Muslim character and actor Mazhar Khan played the Hindu character. He wanted to send out a message of unity and peace to the audience.

Sometimes, things take no time to change for the worse. Up until 1941, Prabhat Film Company was at its peak in Indian cinema...but then all of a sudden it fell into a trap of problems, leading ultimately to its decline.

When there is bitterness in the hearts for each other, it gets difficult to work together as a team. Something similar happened in Prabhat Film Company in 1941. In those circumstances, Shantaram left Prabhat and went to Mumbai where he established Rajkamal Kalamandir.

Prabhat's decline had begun. In 1944, for the last big film by Prabhat studio, *Ramshastri*, it was impossible to find a director and in the film credits—director's name was left blank. Rekha Deshpande explains, 'The plan was for V. Shantaram to direct *Ramshastri*. But by then differences had sprouted in the company, and Shantaram had left the studio. Following which, Damle and Fatehlal had decided to take up the reins of direction. However, by 1943, Damle fell sick and, eventually, died—halting the film in the process. For a long time following his death, there was confusion as to who should direct the rest of the film. Vishram Bedekar who worked for Prabhat at the time, and had already directed *Lakharani* for it, finished *Ramshastri*.'

Even in the period of its decline, Prabhat Film Company launched two people who would go on in future to achieve remarkable heights in Indian cinema. Dev Anand as the lead actor and Guru Dutt as the choreographer in 1946 film, *Hum Ek Hain*.

Just like its contemporaries, Prabhat Film Co. was also affected by World War II.

During the war, people were making money by way of black marketing. To invest that money they turned towards the film industry. Rekha Deshpande says, 'A lot of money started getting invested into the industry, which gave rise to glamour—increasing the remunerations of actors and actresses. The whole production value was increasing, which was not happening at Prabhat. It, as far as production value is concerned, was getting left behind.'

Although Prabhat closed down in 1953 but stepping out of this studio V. Shantaram established Rajkamal Kalamandir in Mumbai and kept Prabhat alive through his films on social issues. But other founders like Vishnupant Damle and S. Fatehlal also gave a film like *Sant Tukaram* to Indian cinema. Ashoke Rane says, 'Shantaram was there for the directorial concept; but for the execution the contribution of the other two was more. Damle and Fatehlal knew their job as well—they could handle the camera perfectly, they were set designers and artists. Damle even took care of the sound department. Together they had an eye for all of that which Shantaram did not have much knowledge of.'

After the talkies came to India, the credit for expanding regional cinema to national cinema goes to only two production houses—New Theatres of Bengal and Prabhat Film Company of Maharashtra. With new stories, artistes and technical innovations they made their cinema so impactful that it got appreciated not just in regional space but all over the country.

Even after shutting down, Prabhat's name continues to be associated with films. The building and infrastructure of the studio is still where it was, standing on which today is the Film and Television Institute of India—the biggest filmmaking institute in India. Anil Damle says, 'In 1955, after the closure of Prabhat got finalized, S.H. Kelkar took over it. The company stayed with him from 1955 to 1960, but he did not get much business out of it. Then in 1960,

Government of India bought that whole land from Kelkar and, in 1961, established Film and Television Institute on it.'

In India, the task of realizing the journey of dreams of cinema was done by only few. Prabhat Film Company, Pune was one of them, which has carved such a place in the heart of Indian cinema that it can never be forgotten.

FILMOGRAPHY

Gopal Krishna (1929)
Khooni Khanjar (1930)
Udaykal (1930)
Maya Machhindra (1932)
Ayodhyecha Raja (1932)
Agnikankan (Branded Oath) (1932)
Sinhagad (1933)
Sairandhri (1933)
Amrit Manthan (1934)
Dharmatma (1935)
Chandrasena (1935)
Amar Jyoti (1936)
Sant Tukaram (1936)
Rajput Ramani (1936)
Kunku (1937)
Duniya Na Mane (1937)
Mera Ladka (1938)
Gopal Krishna (1938)
Manoos (1939)
Aadmi (1939)

Sant Dnyaneshwar (1940)
Padosi (1941)
Das Baje (1942)
Ramshastri (1944)
Chand (1944)

2
NEW THEATRES STUDIO
Pioneers of Playback Singing in Hindi Cinema

Founder: B.N. Sircar (1901–80)

Made 165 brilliant films in 25 years.

The most memorable film being Devdas.

K.L. Saigal and Bimal Roy entered the film industry through New Theatres.

It brought playback singing and Rabindra Sangeet into cinema.

In 1970, B.N. Sircar was honoured with the Dadasaheb Phalke Award.

Indian cinema is known as the world's largest cinema industry and Bollywood—the Hindi film industry—is considered to be the main contributor to this tag. Compared to Bollywood—its big stars, big budgets, national media and mega entertainment—the regional cinema of India appears a little drab. But if there's one Indian language in which internationally acclaimed films have been made and continues to be so, it's Bengali. Satyajit Ray, Mrinal Sen, Ritwik Ghatak, Uttam Kumar, Suchitra Sen, Aparna Sen and Rituparno Ghosh are names known to all. But before all of them, the foundation of cinema in Bengal was laid by New Theatres.

The founder of New Theatres was Birendranath Sircar, the son of the Advocate General of Bengal, Sir N.N. Sircar. In 1901, B.N. Sircar was born in Bhagalpur. After having studied civil engineering from England, he returned to Kolkata and started a business as a civil architect. He soon acquired the contract to build a cinema hall. The name of the theatre was 'Chitra' and it was inaugurated by Netaji Subhas Chandra Bose.

Film journalist and author Shoma A. Chatterji tells us that B.N. Sircar started making films almost by accident, 'He was in his car and when it crossed a cinema theatre, he saw a crowd standing there. He was curious about the long queues, and so, got out of his car to enquire about it. He was told that those people were standing 'to watch cinema'. He was surprised at how willing people were to shell out money and stand in long queues for it. After watching a few films himself, Sircar decided to become a filmmaker.'

B.N. Sircar's journey in films started with the production

of the silent film, *Bhukher Bhojar* in 1930. The film was a flop at the box office. After that, under the banner of International Film Craft, B.N. Sircar made two more silent films with P.N. Roy and Amar Malik. These two were also flops and International Film Craft had to be shut down. Then once again Sircar, P.N. Roy and Amar Malik came together and founded New Theatres on 10 February 1931.

In 1931, after the release of India's first talkie film—*Alam Ara*—the era of silent films began to near its end. In this new period, producers and directors began to look for new kind of plots and stories. B.N. Sircar realized that he was fortunate to be present in the country's mine of literature—Bengal. And in December 1931, New Theatres began its journey with *Dena Paona* (Outstanding Bills) based on the novel by Sarat Chandra Chattopadhyay. It was one of the first talkies of Bengali cinema.

Film historian Moinak Biswas says, 'When cinema began in India, mostly mythological themes were picked for making films. The audience was very familiar as well as fond of epics like the Ramayana and the Mahabharata. With time, as the film business expanded and production increased, filmmakers turned to the abundant Indian literature for stories.'

Failure kept testing B.N. Sircar for a long time. After the two unsuccessful films of International Film Craft, the first five films of New Theatres also proved to be flops at the box office. Amongst these, the one film which is special is *Natir Puja* which was a recording of a play by Rabindranath Tagore of the same name, and in which Tagore was credited as the writer and director.

Shoma A. Chatterji explains the studio, 'When you enter New Theatres' studio you first reach the "Gol Ghar". It stands apart from the studio floors and has an interesting history. Rabindranath Tagore was about to come to the studio to shoot his film *Natir Puja*. He had spoken to Mr Sircar and told him that he wanted to shoot his film in Sircar's studio. He heartily agreed and then began to think where he would seat Tagore. He did not want Tagore to stand in the heat, as there was no air conditioner in those days. So he got the Gol Ghar made within a week. Before Tagore came Gol Ghar was ready, so that he could sit in its cool shade comfortably. When Tagore completed his film and left, Sircar made his own office in the Gol Ghar.

In spite of the failures, B.N. Sircar kept moving forward diligently in his journey of making films. He had made up his mind to keep pursuing until he was rewarded with success. On a ten-acre land in Tollygunge he built a modern film studio, which had all the modern technology of the time.

According to Pinakee Chakraborty, member of board for New Theatres, 'The practice of having a studio was first started by B.N. Sircar because the studio had a lab, all the equipment, cameras—he introduced the Debrie camera in India, he also bought the Tanner Sound machine from Hollywood and for its training he brought William Deming from Hollywood at a salary of three hundred rupees.'

Back then, there were three big filmmaking companies

in India: Sircar's New Theatres, Himansu Rai's Bombay Talkies and V. Shantaram's Prabhat Studios. But the studio system was introduced by New Theatres. Therefore, it had some of the best artistes and technicians there were. Even Prithviraj Kapoor had moved to Kolkata to join the film industry through New Theatres. He was hired at a salary of just ₹300–400 every month.

It may take a while, but hard work and dedication always bears fruit. On 25 September 1932 came New Theatres' first successful film, *Chandidas*, directed by Debaki Bose. With its success, New Theatres gave birth to a new trend. It started making the same film in different languages of the country. In 1932, *Chandidas* was made in Bengali and two years later the same film was made in Hindi. This trend was maintained, in New Theatres, till the very end.

According to Moinak Biswas by the time Chandidas happened, they all had decided that they would make multi-version films. 'So they shot the films simultaneously in different languages, sometimes with non-Bengali actors, if they did not know how to speak Hindi or Urdu. So, in 1935, when P.C. Barua made the biggest cult film of that time, *Devdas*, in the Bengali version he himself played Devdas but in the Hindi version K.L. Saigal was made the hero.'

Devdas was released at Chitra Theatre on 26 April 1935. After watching the film, Sarat Chandra Chattopadhyay himself praised the director, P.C. Barua, and said, 'It appears that I was born to write *Devdas* because you were born to re-create it on cinema,' he adds.

Shoma A. Chatterji believes *Devdas* is timeless because

it has a tragic hero. And when the hero fails, the public likes him more than the two powerful women in the story. She feels, 'Both the women characters are very strong but the story is more about the failure of the man. We do not know what that failure is but if we try to find that out, we realize that more than the story, the attention was given to Devdas' character. People have narrated the same story with their own interpretations far too many times now.' The last she had counted, Chatterji says, there were fourteen film versions of *Devdas*.

Like *Chandidas*, *Devdas* too was made in multiple languages—Telugu, Assamese and Hindi. The Hindi version is what made the actor K.L. Saigal a star.

In the film industry, behind every star is a connoisseur who realizes the potential in an actor to go on to become a star, later. K.L. Saigal too was one such star whose talent was brought to the fore by New Theatres.

Pinakee Chakraborty shares an interesting anecdote about how K.L. Saigal came into films. He says, 'In North Kolkata there was an entertainment programme which R.C. Boral, Amar Malik and Nitin Bose had attended. There they had noticed a singer who also played the harmonium. R.C. Boral liked that song a lot. He told Mr Sircar that he had heard a man singing at the programme and that he should listen to it. The next day, that man was called to the studio and there he sung for B.N. Sircar who liked his singing but said that the fellow should be first trained for acting because he didn't know that at all. So, K.L. Saigal was trained and brought into films in 1931.'

In 1935 after the success of *Devdas*, the golden period of New Theatres began and continued for ten years. During this time, New Theatres produced thirty-eight films which were equally loved by the film critics and the audience. Behind all that success were three directors of New Theatres—P.C. Barua, Nitin Bose and Debaki Bose.

P.C. Barua's first introduction to cinema was in Europe after watching Ernst Lubitsch and Rene Clair's films. Between 1935 and 1940, P.C. Barua made twelve successful films with New Theatres, the best of which was *Devdas*, *Manzil*, *Mukti* and *Adhikar*. In all these films he had brought the technique of that era's European and American cinema.

Shoma Chatterji says, 'If we discuss New Theatres, it is not possible to not talk of P.C. Barua and *Mukti* and there is no one who would not talk about the scene where the door is used as a simile. One after the other the doors open in the scene and the name of the film is *Mukti*, which in the end is freedom for the man as well as the woman. Because the doors used were very wide, Barua used some techniques to make the doors look narrow so that the camera could easily follow through them. It is a beautiful shot which in the language of cinematography is called depth focus.'

P.C. Barua did not just bring technical innovation through his film, but he also developed a new acting style in the cinema of Bengal and Indian cinema by extension, which was natural like the actors in Europe and Hollywood did. According to Somnath Gupta, who directed New Theatres'

2011 National Award winning, *Ami Adu*, says, 'It was P.C. Barua who started this experiment of "no acting". It meant delivering lines in a very simple manner as if they were not acting but only behaving naturally.'

Upper-middle-class was prominently featured in the films of P.C. Barua, along with human relationships, especially the city life and also the issues pertaining to women. However, these were never the focal points of the story, but were used as subtle themes.

The second pillar of the golden period of New Theatres was director Nitin Bose. From a cinematographer he went on to become a director and made impressive films like *President*, *Desher Mati*, *Bhagya Chakra*, *Jeevan Maran* and *Kashinath*. Nitin Bose is known for his experiments with camera and lights. He is also credited for introducing playback singing to Indian cinema, in 1935, in *Bhagya Chakra* (*Dhoop Chhaon* in Hindi).

Pinakee Chakraborty shares another anecdote, 'One day, while the shooting was going on, Nitin Bose went to pick up Pankaj Mullick and saw that Mullick was humming a song which was simultaneously being played on the record. Nitin Bose immediately asked him to pick up his record and come to the studio with him. On reaching, they also called R.C. Boral to join them at the studio and told him they wanted to work on this idea, asking for his opinion. Boral okayed the idea and that day itself playback singing was introduced for the first time.'

The director who gave New Theatres its first success in the form of *Chandidas*, Debaki Bose was the third pillar of the golden era of the studio. Debaki Bose made seven successful films for New Theatres, major amongst which were *Chandidas*, *Vidyapati* and *Nartaki*. Bose is credited for bringing innovations in the field of sound and music through his films.

According to Shoma Chatterji, Bose gave a lot of importance to music: religious hyms were a common feature in his films. 'Words are not enough to express about Debaki Bose. He could adapt to every change. He started with *Shri Chaitanya Mahaprabhu* and other mythological films, then he made *Sagar Sangam* which was not his last film but one of the later ones for which he got President's Award for the Best Film.

In the golden era of New Theatres, music also made its independent place and got a new identity. The music of almost every film by New Theatres became very popular. On the one hand the pillars of New Theatres for direction were P.C. Barua, Nitin Bose and Debaki Bose, on the other for music direction there were R.C. Boral, Pankaj Mullick and Timir Baran whose melodies became the tone and spirit of New Theatres.

Music has had an old tradition in Bengal. The melodies of traditional Bengali music can be heard in all the films of New Theatres. But these music directors added the sounds of Western instruments and gave music a makeover.

Music composer Debojyoti Mishra says, 'Orchestra is of major importance in the films and so are the musicians. Like R.C. Boral had a thirty-piece orchestra, in which Newman Sahib used to play the piano and organ to blend the European music into Indian music. Later on, it was Boral who became the conductor of the orchestra himself. He also understood that in Indian cinema the Indian music cannot work as just music. They would need some different sounds with dramatic moments in the films, like with cello, violin, viola, clarinets—all were needed together, with Indian hyms like keertans and bhajans. So, he started this mixed culture tradition and gave it respect.'

Rabindra Sangeet is an important part of Bengali music. A mix of Indian classical music and folk music, Rabindra Sangeet is said to be the pride of Bengal. New Theatres was the first studio to which Gurudev Rabindranath Tagore gave the permission to use his songs and poems in films.

According to Pinakee Chakraborty, 'P.C. Barua had told Nitin Bose that they would use a little Rabindra Sangeet in a film and they said that they would have to take Gurudev's permission for that. So, one day Bose and Barua went to meet him at Jorasanko Thakur Bari and told him that there was a song in *Mukti*, composed by Pankaj Mullick, which they would like him to listen. Tagore agreed and asked them to bring Mullick to his home. When he heard the song he was so happy that he asked Pankaj Mullick to compose the music for all the lyrics and poems he had written. It was through the film *Mukti* that Rabindra Sangeet was introduced in films.'

New Theatres earned a name for good music, literature-based plots and its good actors. It was established in the days of British Raj, and the social themes regarding the freedom struggle were usually absent in the studio's films.

But it takes only a few incidents to disrupt a good run. The first major hurdle that disrupted the golden period of New Theatres was in 1940 when there was a fire in the studio. And by 1943, World War II also slowed down the film business considerably.

Moinak Biswas tells us that with the onset of World War II a lot more happened, 'It was a difficult period. There was a massive deficiency of raw stock. It started getting rationed. Imports had also been affected, since Indians did not manufacture raw stock, they were dependent on imports. Several other restrictions were introduced during the war. The film studios had a hard time through those years.

New Theatres' journey was not over yet. One of its most talented and well-known face was yet to join. Born in Dhaka in 1909, Bimal Roy started his film career at New Theatres as a camera assistant. Roy released his first directorial in 1944, *Udayer Pathey*, and showed political issues on the screen. According to Somnath Gupta, 'It was the first political Bengali film because he dealt with a theme dependent on two things—class difference and harassment of the poor.'

A major reason for the political scenario to be brought upon the screen was Indian People's Theatre Association (IPTA) which was founded in 1942. Bimal Roy was associated with IPTA and the impression of that is clearly visible in his film. Moinak Biswas says, 'It was in the late 40s when IPTA artistes began migrating to film studio because IPTA was gradually declining. Mid-50s onwards, around 1953–54, if you observe, those who were making the best music, were good lyricists, writing the best scripts and some fantastic directors too had all come from IPTA, which was India's first Left wing cultural movement. Bimal Roy, Salil Chowdhury, Hrishikesh Mukherjee, Ritwik Ghatak had all come from there.

In 1945, New Theatres made the Hindi version of *Udayer Pathey*. The name of the film was *Hamrahi*. This pre-independence film had Rabindranath Tagore's song, 'Jan Gan Man', which post-independence became the national anthem of the country.

A little after World War II, India became independent. But the Partition broke the back of Bengali cinema. Its biggest loss was borne by New Theatres.

Shoma Chatterji says that there was a big gap during the World War II, when no production was done. 'If you trace the history of Bengali cinema, you'll see that this was the point when Bimal Roy and the others were leaving. It was simply because there was no work in Bengal, and they left in search of new horizons. Immensely talented people, like

Nabendu Ghosh and Salil Chowdhury, who were a find of Bimal Roy, all moved to Bombay. There was no production happening in Kolkata and studios were not functioning.'

In 1950, based on the life of Subhas Chandra Bose, *Pehla Admi* was the last film by Bimal Roy for New Theatres. And in 1955 came *Bakul*, which was the last film by New Theatres

For his contribution to Indian cinema, in 1970 the Government of India honoured B.N. Sircar with the Dadasaheb Phalke Award and in 1972, honoured him with the Padmbhushan. Sircar died on 28 November 1980.

Sixty years after the foundation of New Theatres was laid, B.N. Sircar's son, Dilip Sircar, once again revived the banner by making films under it. Shoma Chatterji tells us about it, 'New Theatres made a comeback in 2011 with a film called *Ami Aadu* which even won a National Award for Best Feature Film in Bengali. It was the directorial debut of Somnath Gupta.'

Somnath Gupta tells us that when he went to see Dilip Sircar, it took only one line of the story's narration for Sircar to declare it as unique. He asked Gupta to write the script and to not compromise on his ideas by thinking of the box office. Gupta recalls the words of Dilip Sircar, 'You are making this film under the banner of New Theatres. So keep that in mind while making the film. Don't think whether the film is going to be a hit or not.'

One year after the release of *Ami Aadu*, in 2010, Dilip Sircar also passed away. New Theatres made 165 films in total, and has left such an impression on Bengali and Indian cinema that its influence can still be seen.

Somnath Gupta says, 'National sentiments were given a priority at New Theatres. Right decision was made based on imagination and storyline because if you think about New Theatres, it had become a pioneer in a lot of aspects at that time. It was not just a studio. It had become an institution.'

Shoma Chatterji says, 'Most of the films by the studio proved to be a milestone and today are considered classics. If today one were to write the history of Bengali cinema, most of the New Theatres' films would be a part of it. Not just the ones directed by P.C. Barua, but several others too.'

In the 1930s and 40s, New Theatres of Kolkata, going with its name, gave a chance to numerous new actors, directors, musicians, technicians and writers to showcase their talent. With background music, recording of songs in the studio, films based on popular novels, B.N. Sircar gave such a strong foundation to Bengali cinema that it strengthened the cinema of the whole country. This is why the name, New Theatres, would always be remembered in the history of not just Bengal but of Indian cinema.

FILMOGRAPHY

Dena Paona (1931)
Natir Puja (1932)
Punarjanma (1932)
Chirakumar Sabha (1932)
Pallisamaj (1932)
Chandidas (1932)
Mohabbat Ke Ansu (1932)

Zinda Lash (1932)
Subah Ka Sitara (1932)
Kapalkundala (1933)
Sita (1933)
Rajrani Meera (1933)
Mirabai (1933)
Daku Mansoor (1934)
Ruplekha (1934)
P. Brothers (1934)
Mahua (1934)
Chandidas (1934)
Devdas (1935)
Bhagyachakra (1935)
Manzil (1936)
Grihadaha (1936)
Karodpati a.k.a. Millionaire (1936)
Maya (1936)
President (1937)
Didi (1937)
Mukti (1937)
Vidyapati (1937)
Bidyapati (1938)
Abhagin (1938)
Abhignan (1938)
Desher mati (1938)
Achinpriya (1938)
Sathi (1938)
Street Singer 1938)
Adhikar (1939)

Dushman (1939)
Baradidi (1939)
Sapure (1939)
Rajat Jayanti (1939)
Jiban Maran (1939)
Parajoy (1940)
Daktar (1940)
Abhinetri (1940)
Nartaki (Hindi: 1940) (Bengali: 1941)
Parichoy (1941)
Pratishruti (1941)
Shodhbodh (1942)
Minakshi (1942)
Priyo Bandhabi (1943)
Kashinath (1943)
Dikshul (1943)
Udayer Pathey (1944)
Hamrahi (1945)
Dui Purush (1945)
Biraj Bou (1946)
Nurse Sisi (1947)
Ramer Sumati (1947)
Pratibad (1948)
Anjangarh (1948)
Mantramugdha (1949)
Bishnupriya (1949)
Rupkatha (1950)
Bhagaban Shree Shree Ramkrishna (1955)
Ami Aadu (Aadur Prem) (2011)

3

BOMBAY TALKIES LIMITED

Star Makers

Founders: Devika Rani and Himansu Rai

Established in 1935 in Malad, Mumbai, by Himansu Rai and Devika Rani.

It was a unique collaboration of German and Indian talent.

The first Indian film studio to be listed on the Bombay Stock Exchange.

In 20 years, from 1935 to 1955, they made 102 films.

They introduced Ashok Kumar, Lata Mangeshkar, Dev Anand and Dilip Kumar into the Indian cinema.

In 1970, Devika Rani received the country's first Dadasaheb Phalke Award.

With the arrival of India's first talkie film—*Alam Ara*, the era of silent films ended. There was sound in the films now and that was no less than a revolution back then. With the advent of this path-breaking technology, many studios came up in the film industry, such as Hindustan Films, Star Films, East India Film Company, Majestic Films, Royal Art Studio, Krishna Movietone, Madan Theatre and Wadia Movietone. But only three studios came out as strong pillars: Prabhat Studios in Pune, New Theatres in Bengal and Bombay Talkies in Bombay

And if today Mumbai is known as the birth place and the workplace of Hindi cinema, the reason is the studio where the foundation of Hindi cinema was laid. Established by Devika Rani and Himansu Rai (also Himanshu Rai) in 1935—Bombay Talkies.

According to film historian Ashish Rajadhyaksha, Bombay Talkies is very crucial because it started at a time when we only had the silent cinema with financiers that came from Lahore and even Europe. *The Light of Asia*, the first film that Himansu Rai had made was co-directed by a German Filmmaker called Franz Osten. The trend continued with films like *The Light of Asia*, *Shiraz*, *A Throw of Dice*, *Karma*—until the coming of sound. These were the films before Bombay Talkies.

When Himansu Rai kick-started Bombay Talkies Studio, he had in mind a proper industrial studio. There was corporate money coming in, which is why he had a board of trustees consisting of some very eminent personalities from the Bombay economy scene. Nothing like that had happened before in Bombay.

The founder of Bombay Talkies, Himansu Rai, was born in 1892. In 1920, he got a degree in law from London, but his first love was performing arts. During this time, he met Devika Rani who had studied at the Royal Academy of Dramatic Art and the Royal Academy of Music.

In 1929, after having done a few films together, the couple got married. Both, the husband and wife, were interested in different forms of filmmaking. So, they went to UFA Studios in Germany to learn more about the art.

Writer and historian Amrit Gangar tells us that the first film the German filmmaker Franz Osten and Himansu Rai made was a silent film for Germany's Emelka Studios, *The Light of Asia* (*Prem Sanyas* in Hindi) in 1925. In 1926, they made the second silent film, *Shiraz*. In 1929, they made *A Throw of Dice* (*Prapanch Paas* in Hindi). After three films, Himansu Rai wanted to come to India to try his luck here, and so, he came to Bombay.

In Bombay, an affluent Parsi industrialist named F.E. Dinshaw offered Rai his land in Malad to set up a studio. Both, Rai and Devika Rani, liked the property right away, and established the Bombay Talkies Studio on it in 1934.

They had found a land for the studio but like any other business what they needed first in order to begin work was human resource. Himansu Rai and Devika Rani were extremely influenced by their training in Germany. They wanted Bombay Talkies to be as good as any international production house, state-of-the-art studio. For this reason, Rai asked his good old friend Franz Osten to come and help him make the studio. Osten didn't come alone, he got along some fine crewmen like cinematographer Josef Wirsching, a lab technician, a production designer, and many more such people. It was almost as if Malad had been transformed into a mini Munich.

Bombay Talkies was launched in 1935 in Malad, Mumbai, and it went on to make 120 films in a span of only twenty years. It was the beginning of a new chapter in the world of Hindi cinema.

In 1935, came the first film by Bombay Talkies—*Jawani Ki Hawa*, which was based on a story written by Niranjan Pal and was directed by Franz Osten.

The studio's second film *Achhut Kannya*, starring Devika Rani and Ashok Kumar, released in 1936. It was a love story between a Brahmin boy and an Untouchable girl. It was evident that the film was furthering the drive initiated by Mahatama Gandhi and B.R. Ambedkar. The film had a very strong impact on the audiences and a stupendous box office collection.

'*Achhut Kannya*'s impact was so great that even Jawaharlal Nehru had written a fan mail to Devika Rani', says Nalin Shah, a prominent Hindi film music historian. 'People still remember the song "*Main ban ki chidiya ban ke ban ban bolun re*". Ashok Kumar would insist that he was not a regular singer, but in those days playback singing was not an option—Kumar had to sing out of compulsion. The song may have been simple, almost like a nursery rhyme, but he did not have the confidence to sing it. After fifteen days of rehearsal, Ashok Kumar and Devika Rani managed to sing on the set. One must know that studios were not soundproof back in the day, but the mike was hung from a tree branch so that the lead couple could sing at a fast pace. A lot of hard work went into the song.'

Ashok Rane of Indian Film Academy feels that *Achhut Kannya* was a superhit film because its theme was Untouchability. 'At a time when it was unheard of, the film showed an upper caste man and an Untouchable woman become friends and fall in love. Himansu Rai had dared to pick such a sensitive subject for his film and, fortunately, the audience had liked it a lot. The realistic approach with which the film was made is obvious when you watch it. On the other hand, its contemporaries were made with an extensively dramatic approach that is absent in *Achhut Kannya*.'

From *Achhut Kannya* came the first star of the Hindi film industry—Subodh Kumar Ganguly, better known as Ashok Kumar who, in 1988, was also honoured with the Dadasaheb Phalke Award. But the truth is that Ashok Kumar was in fact reluctant about taking up acting as a career initially.

Nalin Shah tells us that the first Bombay Talkies film made was *Jawani Ki Hawa* in 1935. The hero was supposed to be Najmal Hussain but for some personal reasons he had an argument with Himansu Rai, who then began scouting for a new hero. Rai was then introduced to Ashok Kumar, whom he found decently okay to do the film.

But Ashok Kumar was not ready. He was afraid what

his family would say. Franz Osten took his screen test and rejected him, telling Himansu Rai that he would not do. Osten said that Ashok Kumar looked like a girl, how could he possibly act.

But Himansu Rai was hell-bent on taking him as a hero so a new name was fashioned for him—Ashok Kumar. Ashok Kumar was the first Kumar in the film industry; after him came Raj Kumar, Rajendra Kumar, Dilip Kumar and Manoj Kumar.

The music of *Achhut Kannya* was composed by Saraswati Devi (Khorshed Homji), who continued to work with Bombay Talkies for the next fourteen years. When Homji was asked to compose the music for the film, the Parsis in the country were not in favour of allowing a girl from their community to work in the film industry. They even threatened Himansu Rai in order to deter him from doing so. But Rai was not one to back down. He did get her on board, but for the safety of Khorshed Homji and her sister Manik Homji, who was with her, he changed their names. Khorshed became Saraswati Devi and Manik became Chandra Prabha.

From 1935 to 1943 in every Bombay Talkies' film Ashok Kumar was the lead actor. Paired with him would be Himansu Rai's wife and the most popular actress of the studio—Devika Rani. Amrit Gangar elaborates on Devika Rani, 'She was a well-educated woman and had been trained in the art form in the United Kingdom and Germany. She was related to Nobel Laureate Rabindranath Tagore and was extremely beautiful in person. It was her personality that easily made her stand out in a crowd.'

From 1935 to 1939, the trend of mythological films was coming to an end. Studios were looking for new subjects, new stories. Contemporaries of Bombay Talkies like Prabhat Film Company and New Theatres shifted to making films that captured social issues or films based on literature—such as *Chandidas* (1934), *Dharmatma* (1935) and *Devdas* (1936).

Bombay Talkies tried something very different altogether. They created a new metaphor for their stories. Studio writer Niranjan Pal beautifully threaded love stories in social themes and invented a formula for a commercial Hindi film. For example, *Achhut Kanya* (1936), *Bandhan* (1940) and *Mahal* (1949).

Ashish Rajadhyaksha says, 'Hindi film—as it was understood—is one with a heroine (a village belle who would wear knee-length sarees), a hero (a fellow from a town or city who would come to his country house), and quite a few stereotypes about urban-rural conflicts; this formula was invented by Bombay Talkies.'

It is quite interesting to note that Himansu Rai, Devika Rani and Niranjan Pal were all quite Westernized, but the films by Bombay Talkies were usually set in villages. It's anybody's guess why the villages shown in the films are very different from the actual villages of India.

Amrit Gangar explains the fair scene in *Achhut Kannya*, 'They set up the fair in the studio, arranged everything—

singers, musicians, pitched tents. That set-up of a village fair became a kind of model. An anglicized village can be called an invention of Bombay Talkies.'

By 1939, Bombay Talkies had released sixteen films. Its cast and stories were Indian, the crew German. Emotions were Eastern, techniques were Western. Many experts believe this combination to be the reason behind the success of Bombay Talkies. Its production stages were exactly like how they were in Hollywood then, along with a unique German discipline. The shooting would start at 9.30 a.m. and end at 5.30 p.m. Outdoor shoots were very few and almost everything was shot within the studio. Whether there was any particular work or not, everyone was expected to be on set by 9.30 in the morning. The German disciplined ways collaborated very well with the sentimental and melodramatic Indian mindsets. The kind of romanticism that you have in the Bombay Talkies' films, the kind of social reformative messages that you see in them were born out of this only.

Not just a full-fledged studio which had its own sets, artistes, sound studios, etc., but Bombay Talkies had become a public limited company listed on the Bombay Stock Exchange by 1939. The studio was both artistically and commercially at its peak but look at the irony—it received a rude shock at this juncture. World War II began, and the British Government started arresting the citizens of its enemy countries—Germany and Japan.

Ashok Rane elaborates, 'Franz Osten and all the

cinematographers and other technicians were the backbone of Bombay Talkies. During the World War II, Britain and Germany were on the opposite ends of the war. So, the British Government in India intended to arrest Franz Osten and others. They had to leave, and they did. As soon as they left, Himansu Rai felt handicapped without his technicians and the right people.'

It was a time when the studio had 15–20 films on the floor, which had to be halted. Himansu Rai could not bear the financial and mental loss that had befallen him. He died on 16 May 1940.

But as they say—the show must go on. The Board of Directors handed over the responsibility of the studio to Devika Rani. This eventually lead to the creation of two different groups in the studio. According to Nalin Shah, one group was of Shashadhar Mukerji (also S. Mukerji) which was joined by Ashok Kumar and Kavi Pradeep. Amiya Chakrabarty and Anil Biswas joined Devika Rani's group. They even made films individually: Devika Rani made *Basant*, which was a hit in 1942 and S. Mukerji made *Kismet*, which was a superhit in 1943. *Kismet* had a record of running continuously for three years and eight months in non-stop regular shows.

Amrit Gangar says that these groups were made so that they both managed the studio in their own way. It continued for some time. From the point of view of cinema aesthetics, Devika Rani felt these two groups would work well and provide different dimensions. Amiya Chakrabarty's next film was *Jwar Bhata*, which marked the debut of Dilip Kumar.

From Shashadhar Mukerji's group came *Bandhan* in 1940. Directed by Gyan Mukherjee, the film was a superhit. Infact, Gyan Mukherjee is known as the first formula director of the Hindi cinema who introduced themes like 'crime doesn't pay' and 'boy meets girl', which in the coming years became indispensable ideas for Hindi films.

Kismet was the most successful film of that time of Hindi cinema and continued to be so till 1975 when ultimately Sholay broke its record. *Kismet* established the formula of lost and found so well in Hindi cinema that for years filmmakers used this formula.

Ashok Rane throws light on the contribution of Gyan Mukherjee to Hindi cinema in the form of cult films like *Achhut Kannya*, which too in later years became a formula for commercial film—the formula of anti-hero—a character that was even played by Amitabh Bachchan at one point. The original idea was that a hero should be clean; he shouldn't smoke, shouldn't drink. Then came an anti-hero with *Kismet*. The way Ashok Kumar's character smoked in the film was copied in most films to come. The film ran for five years at Roxy theatre in Mumbai and three-and-a-half years at Roxy in Kolkata.

By 1943, there were a lot of disagreements between the two groups. As a result in that year itself Shashadhar Mukerji along with Ashok Kumar, financier Chunni Lal and director Gyan Mukherjee quit Bombay Talkies and established his own studio—Filmistan. His studio made films like *Nagin*

(1954), *Jagriti* (1954), *Munimji* (1955), *Paying Guest* (1957), *Tumsa Nahi Dekha* (1957), etc.

'Devika Rani may have been the captain of the ship, but there were others on board too. And they had their own ambitions to fulfil,' says Ashok Rane, 'Just as S. Mukerji established Filmistan and took Ashok Kumar along with him, there were many others who became studio owners or film producers. People left Bombay Talkies to follow their own dreams. It's a very common practice in the film industry, even today—to assist others in the first few years of their career, but eventually everyone moves on to start something of their own.'

Bombay Talkies was then left to the care of Devika Rani and Amiya Chakrabarty. In 1944, they released *Jwar Bhata* which did not do any wonders at the box office but it marks the debut of Dilip Kumar, who went on to become a big star of Hindi cinema.

The story goes that once when Devika Rani and Rajnarayan Dubey were driving back from Nasik to Bombay, they halted at a military camp in Devlali which had a canteen. Dilip Kumar was the manager there—a good-looking, young and smart chap. They immediately found him to be a good fit for films and made him an offer.

Pratima, which came in 1945, was Devika Rani's last film as a producer. By now she had lost interest in the studio. She sold the majority of her shares to the owner of Famous Studios, Shiraz Ali Hakim, and bid goodbye to Bombay Talkies.

By 1945, all the old hands of Bombay Talkies had left the studio—disintegrating it completely. During this time many other public-listed companies began to break down. It was evident that World War II had changed the future of the studio system and Indian cinema.

Ashish Rajadhyaksha says, 'Economically-speaking, the impact of World War II was bigger than Independence. The city of Bombay had an entire economic structure which was associated with the industrialists and the trading classes. They were often the kind of people who invested into the film industry. After the War ended, a huge amount of money came into the film industry—creating a new kind of economy, which was what caused the studios to shut down. A new structure was formed in the film industry, where people would make individual films rather than having huge overheads and infrastructures to run complete studios, which was unsustainable after the War.'

When the Partition happened, the stakeholder of the majority of the shares of Bombay Talkies, Shiraz Ali Hakim, left for Pakistan. People felt that was the end for Bombay Talkies. But then a businessman, Govindram Seksaria, bought the studio and brought Ashok Kumar back.

The studio then gave some memorable films like *Ziddi* in 1948, which was the first big success of the then rising star Dev Anand. It also marked the rise of Lata Mangeshkar as a playback singer in the Hindi film industry. Before *Ziddi*, she had been struggling because no producer was willing to take her. Both Chandulal Shah of Ranjit Movitone and S. Mukerji of Filmistan had rejected her voice, outright. It was music directors Khemchand Prakash and Master Ghulam Haidar who had given her a break in Bombay Talkies.

Post-1949, with successes like *Mahal* and *Sangram*, it appeared that the studio had once again come alive. However, in 1950 Ashok Kumar once more quit the studio and as a result Bombay Talkies was again left directionless. It got buried in debt. *Baadbaan* (1954) was its last film, after which the studio shut down.

Not just for its films, but Bombay Talkies studio is today remembered for its two major contributions to Indian cinema: technical finesse of international standards; and for introducing 280 artistes—actors, writers, directors, cameramen, producers and sound recordists—who in later years became the pillars of Hindi cinema.

Talking about its contribution, Amrit Gangar says, 'Bombay Talkies was like a school, a university where you could learn. Raj Kapoor was a clapper boy there. Dev Anand entered the industry through it. Then there was Madhubala: she actually used to live there, in the same area, and was known as Baby Mumtaz. Then there was Leela Chitnis who became a star with the studio. So they all got something or the other out of Bombay Talkies—a sense of filmmaking: how a film is made, produced...because Bombay Talkies was not just a commercial enterprise but a place to learn.

Apart from this huge contribution, Bombay Talkies was the first such studio of the country where assembly line production of films used to happen. It was here that the model of producer, distributer and exhibitor first took birth. The work ethic of Bombay Talkies Studio was not just an inspiration for that time but continues to be so even today. The work used to start at sharp 9.30 a.m. and pack up at sharp 5.30 p.m. This is where a wonderful amalgamation of Indian feelings and German discipline was seen for the first and the last time. Because of all this, Bombay Talkies is remembered today as the land from where the *khwaabon ka safar* of Hindi cinema began.

FILMOGRAPHY

Jawani ki Hawa (1935)
Achhut Kannya (1936)
Janmabhumi (1936)
Jeevan Naiya (1936)
Mamta and Miya Biwi (1936)
Izzat (1937)
Jeevan Prabhat (1937)
Prem Kahani (1937)
Savitri (1937)
Bhabhi (1938)
Nirmala (1938)
Vachan (1938)
Durga (1939)
Kangan (1939)
Bandhan (1940)
Jhoola (1941)
Kismet (1943)
Char Ankhen (1944)
Jwar Bhata (1944)

Pratima (1945)
Milan (1946)
Nateeja (1947)
Majboor (1948)
Ziddi (1948)
Mahal (1949)
Sangram (1950)
Mashaal (1950)
Maa (1952)
Tamasha (1952)
Baadbaan (1954)

4

RAJKAMAL KALAMANDIR

Content over Celebrities

Founder: V. Shantaram (1921–90)

Located in Mumbai's Lower Parel.

The backdrop of the studio has been Indianness, Marathi ethos and rural background. An important role was played by drama and music, technical evolution of cinema and freedom from the 'star system'.

It has won five National Awards and a Silver Bear at the Berlin Film Festival.

Cinema is such an art form where there is a confluence of many different art forms: architecture, photography, theatre, music, dance, acting, literature and poetry. It is also a confluence of inferences which sometimes come from their native regions and at other times from foreign lands.

In the early years of Hindi cinema, the influence of Western cinema can be easily spotted: Charlie Chaplin's in R.K. Studio, German Expressionism in Bombay Talkies, Hollywood Noir films in Navketan Films and Guru Dutt's films. Amongst these rose a studio which was miles away from the Western influences. This studio made Indian culture and its civilization, literature and music its foundation, and in its journey of fifty years always remained deeply attached to its roots—this was Rajkamal Kalamandir.

In 1896, for the first time the Lumière brothers of France exhibited moving pictures with the help of a cinematograph projector which gave birth to the word 'movie'. Thus came cinema in existence, and exactly five years later on 18 November 1901 in India was born a great personality who maintained the pride of Hindi and Marathi cinema in the coming seventy-two years—Shantaram Rajaram Vankudre or V. Shantaram, fondly known as Anna Saheb.

V. Shantaram's father Rajaram used to supply petromax lamps to a drama troupe in Kolhapur. Thus, Shantaram's childhood was spent around Marathi theatre. Later, from 1920 to 1928, Shantaram learnt the skills of film production while working on silent movies at Baburao Painter's Maharasthtra Film Company in Pune. In 1929, along with Keshavrao Dhaipar, Vishnupant Dhamle and S. Fatehlal, Shantaram started Prabhat Film Company.

And this was where the foundation for V. Shantaram's

filmmaking style was laid.

Actor and director Sachin Pilgaonkar says, 'Initially they were four partners, then they became five. But everyone was making films. While all mythological and historical films were made by others, the films which had social elements were all made by Shantaram Bapu.'

By 1942, Anna Saheb had covered the journey from silent movies to talkies with Prabhat Films. He was now considered amongst the most capable directors in India. Some people believe that maybe he had a desire to breakout of the boundaries of Prabhat or a passion to carve a separate identity for which Shantaram left the production house. So, Shantaram hired the land of Wadia Studio on lease from A.H. Wadia in Mumbai, Lower Parel, and laid the foundation of Rajkamal Kalamandir Studio.

Kiran Shantaram, son of V. Shantaram, says: 'Anna Saheb was an expert at picking up titles and names. Anna Saheb's father's name was Rajaram and his mother's name was Kamal. So he made a combination of both and chose the name "Rajkamal". "Kalamandir" was added because it was the place for artistes and thus was a mandir (temple) related to kala (art).'

It could be the influence of all the years spent at Prabhat Studios or his love for his culture and literature because of which Shantaram chose a mythological subject for the first film released by the studio in 1943—*Shakuntala*.

Shakuntala was such a big hit that it completed 104

weeks at Swastik Theatres, Lemington Road, Mumbai. Even till the time Rajkamal's third film released, the shows of *Shakuntala* would be houseful. Its success gave Rajkamal the freedom to choose a story which was an absolutely new experience to cinema viewers at that time: a biopic—*Dr. Kotnis Ki Amar Kahani*.

Kiran Shantaram tells us the background story: 'Four Indian doctors were chosen and sent on a medical mission to China (including Dr Dwarkanath Kotnis). Writer K.A. Abbas had published Dr Kotnis' biography titled *And One Did Not Come Back* in 1944. Anna Saheb read that book and decided to make the film on Dr Kotnis.'

There is immense similarity among the four actors in the film and the characters they played in it (the four men sent on the mission to China). If you look at their photographs you'll realize that they resembled the original doctors in their appearance. This was the reason why Dr Kotnis' role was played by V. Shantaram himself.

The year was 1946. The cry for 'swadesh' was echoing in every household. Shantaram was a diehard patriot. In 1942, he had resigned as Honorary Chief Producer from the British Government's Film Advisory Board. *Dr Kotnis...* was Rajkamal Kalamandir's message for a new India.

Author and film historian Rekha Deshpande says, 'Dr Kotnis had gone to China under a plan of the British Government and on that Shantaram had made the biopic. But as was his ideology, he never missed giving a message of patriotism in his films.'

Dr Kotnis' was an Indian story but its appeal was

universal. The film was re-edited for the international audience. The famous American company Mayer & Burstyn, which had also released the Italian film *Bicycle Thief*, distributed *Dr. Kotnis...* in America.

As mentioned earlier, initially the studio land was on lease but with the success of *Dr. Kotnis...* Shantaram paid ₹12 lakh and bought the entire Wadia Studios land. Rajkamal Kalamandir was then a full-fledged studio, with its own Plaza Cinema in Dadar, Mumbai; a distribution company called Silver Screen Exchange; and the first film institute of Asia—Film Academy of India, where they taught a two-year course in filmmaking and a three-year course in motion pictures production.

Kiran Shantaram adds, 'Anna Saheb used to say that an independent producer should always be able to stand independently, that's how he himself worked. And if we take a look at all the bigwigs of his time, like Raj Kapoor, Bimal Roy, Mehboob Khan—they all had production companies and studios. But Rajkamal Studios, when it had started, also had a black-and-white lab. It had its own stills department, poster department, showcards department—which were used in earlier days in cinema halls. So anything and everything that was connected to production of films was readily available at Rajkamal Studios.

From 1947 to 1954, most Rajkamal films tried to spread social messages. In 1947 released *Jeevan Yatra* on the theme of national integration; in 1949, *Apna Desh* made a statement against black market and corruption; in 1950, *Dahej* strongly objected to the dowry system; and in 1953, *Teen Batti Chaar Rasta* talked of social harmony.

Film director Shyam Benegal says, 'Most of the films that Shantaram made depicted the social, economic and political circumstances of India. So the kind of films they made were always socially relevant. They did have entertainment, of course, but look at the kind of films that he made about widow remarriage or the caste system.'

All those things that he showed onscreen were social reform movements in a way. These had taken roots in Maharashtra before they spread to other parts of India because Maharashtra was a very progressive Indian state, socially speaking, since it had its own leaders and their influence was very much there in cinema. It was Shantaram who represented many of these things in cinema.

State Reorganization Act 1956 divided the states on the basis of language, following which the regional cinema started getting subsidies from their states and producers from there started making films in their native language. But prior to this, New Theatres, AVM and Rajkamal were some such names which were already making films not just in their native languages but in Hindi too.

Sachin Pilgaonkar feels that Shantaram made a crossover as he didn't want to limit himself to one language or region, 'He thought why should he stay restricted to just Marathi films? Why should he not make films in Hindi too…so that it spreads all over India, and then even go outside of India,' says Pilgaonkar.

By 1950, Rajkamal Studios had 260 employees, equipment, recording studios and obviously to run such a huge studio apparatus they needed a big commercial hit. Thus, in 1955 came *Jhanak Jhanak Payal Baaje*—a film which was far from the studio's last few socially oriented films: an out-an-out musical, a love story of two dancers, which did not have the agenda of propagating any philosophy or ideology, but was only pure entertainment.

According to film historian Sudhir Nandgaonkar, Shantaram's last 4–5 films before *Jhanak Jhanak Payal Baaje* had flopped. 'Of all the good films in Shantaram's career, *Jhanak Jhanak Payal Baaje* has the weakest story. There was nothing special in its storyline, unlike *Do Ankhen Barah Haath* or *Navrang* or *Duniya Na Mane*. But he wanted to make a successful box office film. He chose a story accordingly and brought the grandeur it requires.'

'It took two years to make that film,' says Kiran Shantaram. 'This was from 1954–55. The film's production costs were very high, Anna Saheb had never made such an expensive film until then. He mortgaged his wife's jewellery and his studio to make that film. By God's grace, the film was such a big hit that everything came back to us.'

In the year 1955, after *Shree 420* and *Azad*, *Jhanak Jhanak Payal Baaje* became the third biggest hit of the year. After such a huge success people felt that Rajkamal would probably make more films on a similar theme but the studio was going to prove everyone wrong.

It is said that history repeats itself. Hollywood director Steven Spielberg's film based on the Holocaust, *Schindler's*

List, which came in 1993, was shot completely in black and white in the time of colour cinema as Spielberg wanted to give the film a documentary-like feel. Very few people know that thirty-six years prior to this, Rajkamal had taken a similar decision in Hindi cinema. He made *Do Ankhen Barah Haath*, a story of prison reform experiment, deliberately in black and white. It was released in India in 1957 and worldwide in 1958, and became the most famous film made by Rajkamal Studios.

According to Kiran Shantaram, the film was based on a real life story. 'Such an experiment had actually undertaken in Aundh, near Satara in Maharasthtra, where prisoners were kept in an open prison on trial basis. When Anna Saheb heard this story, he decided to make it into a film. He asked noted Marathi writer G.D. Madgulkar to start writing the script. Anna Saheb had already made *Jhanak Jhanak Payal Baaje* before this film. So when the final narration took place, the studio's technicians asked Anna Saheb as to why he wanted to make *Do Ankhen Barah Haath* in black and white. And Anna Saheb explained that the beauty of the subject could only come in black and white, and not in colour.'

Sudhir Nandgaonkar says, '...though Gandhiji was not mentioned in the film, it was based on his thought. Gandhiji's belief that "you can change a person" is used there. But Gandhiji's name is nowhere in the film as Shantaram did not want to make it a propaganda. He wanted to only make a film.'

Great art requires great dedication. Taking up the jailor's

role in the film himself, Shantaram had to act in the climax scene which showed a bull fight. Had it been any other producer, director, or actor, he/she would not have taken such a risk, but Shantaram's passion for films was something else. As a result of this scene, Shantaram narrowly escaped losing his eyesight. But he ended up giving Hindi cinema a new outlook towards films. In 1957, the film got the National Award for the Best Feature Film, as well as the Best Feature Film in Hindi.

According to Sudhir Nandgaonkar, 'That film won a Silver Medal at the Berlin International Film Festival in 1958. It was the same year when the Golden Bear Award had gone to Ingmar Bergman and the Silver Bear (Extraordinary Prize by the Jury) was given to V. Shantaram for *Do Ankhen Barah Haath*. Since then no Hindi film has ever received an award at the Berlin Film Festival. With this film, Rajkamal Studios once again proved that cinema is not restricted to any particular region or country, instead it speaks a universal language.'

Kiran Shantaram gives us further anecdotes on this. 'While the film was running in the cinema halls, the prayer song in it, *Aye Maalik Tere Bande Hum*, was being played as a prayer in the schools of Pakistan. People wrote letters to Anna Saheb from across the border saying that the prayer that he had created was great and was being sung in Pakistani schools.'

By the end of the 50s, there came a change in the mindsets

of the film viewers. The era of socially relevant films was almost coming to an end. In the changing times, Rajkamal's films too changed their tune to suit the audience preferences.

V. Shantaram was a far-sighted man. He was the first in the film business to comprehend that the audience's taste had shifted from movies on social reform towards popcorn entertainment.

Guru Dutt's commercial love story *Chaudhavin Ka Chand* came in 1962, Raj Kapoor's *Sangam* came in 1964. But before all of them in 1959, came Rajkamal Kalamandir's most expensive film of the time (with an investment of ₹30 lakh)—*Navrang*.

Music historian Rajiv Vijayakar says, '*Navrang* was to Rajkamal, what *Guide* was for Navketan. It is a benchmark of the creative peak. They also made *Geet Gaaya Pattharon Ne* and *Jal Bin Machhli Nritya Bin Bijli*, which were also a success. Many of his Marathi films had also done well. But *Navrang* was the tip of his creative mountain.'

According to Sudhir Nandgaonkar, *Navrang* was based on the life of Prabhakar, the famous Marathi poet. He says, 'Shantaram wanted to see if a poet's imagination can be captured in a film. Actually imagination is something which we can only have in our minds, we cannot photograph it. But he wanted to do that. And he did it. In *Navrang*, the hero's wife and the character in his imagination have been shown as the same woman.'

In *Navrang*, Rajkamal Kalamandir tried new experiments for song picturization. The story had its base in Maharashtra, but the success of *Navrang* all over the country was owing to its song picturization and music. The film's music composer was C. Ramchandran, who took over from Vasant Desai in Rajkamal Kalamandir.

According to Rajiv Vijayakar, 'C. Ramchandran was among the top five composers of that time. Shantaram left Vasant Desai, who was a huge talent in himself and quite a name in Marathi films too, and went to C. Ramchandran. There he experimented with an upcoming singer like Mahindra Kapoor.' Vijayakar also says that Mahindra Kapoor believed that had it not been for *Navrang*, Shankar-Jaikishan would have never given him a song to sing, 'Shankarji had clearly said to him that they had given him a song only because he had Anna Saheb's reference, who was a father figure in the duo's lives.'

Some people believe that such grandeur was seen only once before *Navrang*, and that was in Raj Kapoor's 1951 film *Awara*. Sachin Pilgaonkar adds, 'Anna always liked grandeur and his films definitely had it. The music was made accordingly so that it could be picturized and presented in magnificence. In the song "*Aadha Hai Chandrama Raat Aadhi*", all the matkas (earthen pots) were not stuck together, but simple kept one over the other. The actress had to perform while balancing it. And then he had displayed huge bells in the same film, sitting on which the artiste had to sway. Raj Kapoor had specially come to Rajkamal to see that set. There was a lot of excitement for it and people would come from all over to see just that.'

Navrang was one of the top five hits of 1959. This film celebrated its silver jubilee in Liberty Cinema, Mumbai. But the success of *Navrang* was never recreated in the studio. In the 60s, natural acting, West-influenced music, shoots in foreign locations and other such new elements were coming into cinema. But the tone of the stories told by Rajkamal Kalamandir remained as dramatic as ever.

According to Rekha Deshpande, 'As far as Hindi cinema is concerned, there is no doubt that in its later days Shantaram was left behind the prevalent time. It is difficult to change the ideology of a man completely. It is usually so deep-rooted that he believes it to be always correct. He can see that the world is changing but he cannot accustom himself to the changing times.'

Probably, this is the reason why in his later films, the music was still great but the films weren't so successful. Nandgaonkar explains, 'In his later works he was copying himself. You can see a copy of *Jhanak Jhanak...* in the dances of *Jal Bin Machhli...* though the stories are a little different. In the life of every artiste, there is a morning, evening and night. *Jal Bin Machhli...* was the evening. The graph had dropped down after *Navrang*, except in his Marathi films where *Pinjra* had soared it up. Otherwise, it was his lean period. He had a studio and he kept making films according to his own sensibilities. But they did not have the charm that *Navrang* or *Do Ankhen...* did.

Shantaram was about to enter the sixth decade of his life. By 1959, he had directed thirty-five films in total for Maharashtra Film Company, Prabhat Studios and Rajkamal

Kalamandir, and he probably got creatively exhausted. This is possibly why Rajkamal Kalamandir could never again make a *Dr. Kotnis ki Amar Kahani*, *Dahej* or *Do Ankhen Barah Haath*.

In the 70s, Rajkamal brought forth only two films: *Jal Bin Machhli Nritya Bin Bijli* in 1971 and the critically acclaimed Marathi film *Pinjra* which released in 1972. That year *Pinjra* won the National Award for Best Feature Film in Marathi.

Rekha Deshpande informs us that films, like *Raja Nene Raja Paranjpe*, which came in the 50s, were very popular in Maharashtra then. The themes revolved around middle-class city life or rural life and most of them would be commercially successful. But later, in competition with Hindi films, they could not last. When *Pinjra* released, Marathi cinema was already in a very bad shape. At a time when Marathi cinema was losing its impact on the Marathi audience, *Pinjra* raised a new hope for it.

From 1972 to 1986, for fourteen years the production house did not produce any film. During this time Rajkamal Kalamandir was known more as a studio for-hire. In fact, many famous scenes and the climax of the 1975 cult film *Deewar* were shot here. The studio's last film under V. Shantaram's direction was *Jhanjhar*, which came in 1986. It is said that by making this film Shantaram had kept his promise of launching his grandson, Sushant Ray. Sadly, by then both Shantaram and Rajkamal's grip on the audience was over. Like other studios of its time Rajkamal Kalamandir also came down to a one-man show.

Sachin Pilgaonkar also feels the same way, 'It definitely was a one-man show. At Rajkamal, everything began and ended with Anna Saheb. Nobody else had the courage to ask for things their way. Everything would happen only the way Anna Saheb wanted it, the others would just follow him and his words.' He adds, 'Sometimes, the name of a man becomes so big that it is impossible to have a bigger name. It is not the case with just Anna Saheb, there are several other names in the film industry which became so big that all their descendents could not go beyond that name. He thought it right to maintain that name, which again was a big responsibility in itself.'

There is an end to every journey but three aspects of Rajkamal Kalamandir make its journey in Hindi cinema even more precious. The first being the development of the technique of filmmaking. Shantaram understood it from the very beginning that in cinema, technique and technical knowledge are important pillars.

According to Sudhir Nandgaonkar, 'Shantaram was the first director to understand that cinema is a technical medium. For this reason, he built a recording studio and other such parts of Rajkamal. He would be among the firsts to buy any new filmmaking technology that would come into the market, it was his speciality. It was he who had taken the first close-up shot with a telephoto lens, which was spread on the whole screen in *Amrit Manthan* (1934).'

Kiran Shantaram tells us that Shantaram's *Pinjra* was the first colour film in Marathi, and after it all others followed suit, 'It was his hobby, he always wanted to be the first to try out new things. For example, *Jal Bin Machhli Nritya Bin Bijli* was the first film that had stereophonic sound.'

The second aspect was to give priority to Indian ethos. Shantaram always chose his story from Indian and Marathi literature. Rekha Deshpande explains, 'Shantaram was born and brought up in India. Unlike Himansu Rai, he did not learn filmmaking in a foreign country. He was learning everything here on his own, he did his own innovation to the devices and that is how he grasped filmmaking and built his own studio. So, his ideology reflected in his cinema and you can see firm depictions of Indian mindset.'

Third aspect was that if Rajkamal Kalamandir was dependent on technology and innovation, it was absolutely free from another factor—the star system. Sudhir Nandgaonkar elaborates on this, 'When Shantaram cast Mahipal in *Navrang*, he was nothing; just a hero in C-grade mythological films. But he found him good enough to play the poet in the film and casted him. Shantaram never believed in the star system. He believed he could extract quality out of whoever came to him. This is the reason why Rajkamal saw several debuts.' Kiran Shantaram tells us that Anna Saheb believed that the audience finds new artistes more relatable to the characters onscreen. That is why he never worked with big artistes.

Shantaram's stature and position in Indian cinema can be understood from the fact that he is known as 'chatrapati' in Marathi cinema. In 1985, he was honoured with the highest Indian award in the field of cinema, Dadasaheb

Phalke Award. After giving seventy-two years to Hindi and Marathi cinema, he died in 1990.

Rajkamal Kalamandir still exists in Mumbai's Lower Parel. It may not be making films today but continues to be regarded highly for its tremendous technical contribution to cinema, for bringing Indian culture and regional tradition to the forefront, and especially for making its own films without any big stars. For these reasons and more, Rajkamal Kalamandir will never be forgotten.

FILMOGRAPHY

Shakuntala (1943)
Parbat Pe Apna Dera (1944)
Dr. Kotnis Ki Amar Kahani (1946)
Lokshahir Ram Joshi (1947)
Apna Desh (1949)
Dahej (1950)
Amar Bhoopali (1951)
Parchhain (1952)
Teen Batti Char Raasta (1953)
Surang (1953)
Subah Ka Tara (1954)
Jhanak Jhanak Paayal Baaje (1955)
Toofan Aur Deeya (1956)
Do Ankhen Barah Haath (1958)
Navrang (1959)
Stree (1961)
Sehra (1963)

Geet Gaya Patharon Ne (1964)
Ladki Sahyadri Ki (1966)
Boond Jo Ban Gayee Moti (1967)
Jal Bin Machhli Nritya Bin Bijli (1971)
Pinjra (1972)
Jhanjhaar (1987)

5

FILMISTAN STUDIO

Cinema is for Entertainment

Founder: Shashadhar Mukerji (1943–1968, also known as S. Mukherjee)

Presently in Goregaon, Mumbai.

The studio made 27 films in 15 years.

Known for its escapist cinema and gave birth to Hindi formula films.

Many big stars got germinated from the studio like Dilip Kumar, Vyjayanthimala and Kishore Kumar. This is also where Shammi Kapoor's iconic style was born.

And the biggest pillar was a name now lost in the pages of history—Shashadhar Mukerji.

If the audience is able to find the colours of their life in the story of a film and its characters, then that establishes the film and its actors in their heart.

When we think of films from 1930 to 1960, we think of names like Raj Kapoor, Dev Anand, Ashok Kumar, Dilip Kumar, Guru Dutt, Madhubala, Meena Kumari, Waheeda Rehman et al. But in that same period, there were some others who gave life to Hindi cinema from behind the curtains. One such name is of Shashadhar Mukerji, who started his own journey with Bombay Talkies but in 1943 founded Filmistan Studio.

Film journalist Ajay Brahmatmaj says, 'When Devika Rani's interest in making films was diminishing and Bombay Talkies was disintegrating, it was getting difficult for others to work in a place where the Head herself was almost inactive. Whether it was Ashok Kumar exiting Bombay Talkies or Shashadhar Mukerji doing the same to establish Filmistan—it was all because they had realized that the studio wasn't working anymore and thought it better to build their own and start work with a new energy.'

Established in 1943, at the peak of the freedom movement, Filmistan produced an amazing variety of films. From the beginning itself, Shashadhar Mukerji never tied the studio to any particular genre. Since its establishment, Filmistan's motto was only entertainment.

Ajay Brahmatmaj adds, 'What today is called the "Bollywood Cinema" which has achieved all heights of popularity in the last twenty years, and the 'special formula' which we believe the films should have were all kick-started by Shashadhar Mukerji, which do not have to do anything with socialism. Their films used to have a simple story where the audience would be entertained, and along with it they would learn a thing or two of importance which was an add-on.'

In actress and Shashadhar Mukerji's grandaughter Tanishaa Mukerji's own words, 'Dada was a very progressive producer. It was a time in our country when all the serious films talking about patriotism and social issues were being made; but when the atmosphere gets intense, when there is a lot of social upheaval, that's when people need a change, and my grandfather pre-empted that. The audience wanted to go to a theatre and escape to another world for those 2–3 hours. So, he observed that and made films for that audience.'

Shashadhar Mukerji made many hit films with Bombay Talkies. After a long success streak, a new beginning comes with its own pressures. He took the studio of Sharda Film Company in Goregaon, Mumbai on lease and with the hit team of *Kismet*—director Gyan Mukerji and actor Ashok Kumar—released the first film of his new studio, *Chal Chal Re Naujawan* in 1944.

According to Film Producer Amit Khanna, 'Shashadhar Mukerji bought the present Filmistan studio in the early 50s, with a bit of private funding from Bhavani Investors. He got that because all his people had a good track record—Ashok Kumar was a big star, Gyan Mukerji was a successful director and he himself was a successful film producer—this team was a strong one.'

Film historian and writer Amrit Gangar states, '*Chal Chal Re Naujawan* had the dream pair of Naseem Banu and Ashok Kumar, and it was made by S. Mukerji—but it flopped.'

This was also the time when the golden period of Bengali cinema was approaching its end. All its big names were moving to Mumbai, and Filmistan used this opportunity to absorb all that talent. Therefore, Nitin Bose, who had come from New Theatres, directed the second film by Filmistan—*Mazdoor* (1945). The very next year, another Bengali joined the studio—S.D. Burman.

'After *Chal Chal Re Naujawan*, they made *Shikari* which became a hit. In that they cast a Parsi actress from Karachi, called Veera and a musician from Bengal who later went on to become a great musician—Sachin Dev Burman. His coming to Filmistan was an important milestone,' adds Amrit Gangar.

Many people believe that this was the time when the birth of a star system took place in the Indian film industry and stars started asking for huge payments to work in films.

Ajay Brahmatmaj reveals, 'People who worked for the studio were on a fixed payroll whether they would be doing three films in a year or four for the studio, such was the norm.' But then came a star who began asking for high remuneration separately for each film. 'Dilip Kumar was the first to break the norm because he was in demand the most, and he knew that people were willing to spend their money on him,' adds Brahmatmaj.

When Filmistan's big star, Ashok Kumar, left the studio in 1947 due to some internal reasons and joined Bombay Talkies, the studio had a major void. Filmistan now needed a new star which was fulfilled by the rising star of the time—Dilip Kumar, who featured in the studio's 1948 hit film, *Nadiya Ke Paar*.

Tanishaa Mukerji recalls how Dilip Kumar was a regular visitor to their house. There would be queues of people outside the house. All the hopefuls would stand there asking for work in the studio's films. Dilip Kumar stood in it too for days, without fail, until one day when S. Mukerji spotted him and said, 'Come in'.

Dilip Kumar's *Shaheed* released the same year as *Nadiya Ke Paar*. Produced by Filmistan in 1948, *Shaheed* earned ₹75 lakh and became the biggest hit of that year. With *Shaheed*, its hero, Dilip Kumar, became the biggest star of that time.

Ajay Brahmatmaj says, 'A feeling of patriotism came forth in that film and such films were required at that time where we could assert ourselves and move ahead remembering our country. So, the film came out at the most opportune time and people accepted it warmly, this got Dilip Kumar his stardom. We have all seen how Dilip Kumar's fame escalated and strengthened his stardom. The special thing about Dilip Kumar, which later happened to Shahrukh Khan too, is that they always got the big opportunities and they proved themselves up to it.'

Filmistan was giving birth to new stars with its new films. Music was a major factor behind the success of these films, and Filmistan was always on the look-out for new talent in the field of music. S.D. Burman was already a part of their journey, soon two others also joined in—C. Ramchandran and Hemant Kumar.

According to Ajay Brahmatmaj, 'When Filmistan was made, Shashadhar Mukerji took an interest in all its aspects. When he came across good music composers and lyricists, he hosted "music-sittings" where they discussed all things music—what kind of music goes in which film and which might become popular. They would fix the number of songs needed in a film, some films would have eight to ten songs in fact.'

Rono Mukerji, son of Shashadhar Mukerji, says that his father was in love with music, 'All the songs of his films for Bombay Talkies and Filmistan were hits. Look at any film of his—for instance, *Shabnam*, the music of which was given by S.D. Burman. His song "*Ye Duniya Roop Ki Chor/ Sun Le Mere Babu*" was very popular. Such were the kinds of songs he had in his films.'

Hemant Kumar who had come from Bengal, marked his debut in the Hindi film industry by composing the music for *Anand Math* of Filmistan. It's noteworthy that Bankim Chandra's 'Vande Mataram', which was declared the national song just two years prior, was heard for the first time in Hindi cinema in that film.

Just as any good Hindi film has a twist, so did Filmistan Studios in the year 1950. Shashadhar Mukerji sold his shares of Filmistan to Tolaram Jalan—a successful businessman who wanted to try his luck in films. Shashadhar Mukherji took a break from films and went off to England. Tolaram Jalan took over the making of films at the studio.

Ajay Brahmatmaj says, 'The reason which seems most plausible is creative tiredness—Shashadar Mukerji probably got tired doing the same kind of work over and over again. Jalan was not a producer, while Shashadhar Mukerji was a truly creative producer. Jalan's interest was purely in the money. It is unfortunate that whenever a businessman steps into this field he feels that it is something which he can easily manage. But eventually he fails because the creative finesse can only come from a creative mind. With money you can buy talent, but cannot identify the better talents.'

Rono Mukerji adds, 'A time came when all the studios were shutting down one after the other. Although in trouble, Filmistan was the only studio which kept running. Tolaram Jalan made eight flop films after buying the studio from S. Mukerji, but he never complained. S. Mukherji though was pretty disheartened by it.'

How can someone whose life is bound to films stay away from it for long? After two years, Shashadhar Mukerji returned, and once again connected with films beginning with *Anarkali* in 1953. It was the biggest hit of 1953.

Ajay Brahmatmaj explains, '*Anarkali* was a fictitious character. There was never any empress in the Mughal Empire whose name was Anarkali. Later on, people tried to find evidence and add things up, but could never find anything concrete. But it was seen as an amazing love story. Moreover, somewhere that tradition was already coming along in Hindi films where a rich guy and a poor girl or a city guy and a village belle were often portrayed in love with each other. What was shown in *Mughal-e-Azam* was an extended portrayal of the same where an emperor falls in love with a courtesan.'

The superhit *Anarkali* introduced two big stars—writer Nasir Hussain who went on to become a big film director; and the prominent Bengali actor, Pradeep Kumar, who attained stardom overnight in Hindi cinema with this film.

A good producer is one who knows how to reap benefits from past successes, and Shashadhar Mukerji did just that in Filmistan. The studio repeated Pradeep Kumar in its next film, *Nagin*, which went on to become an even bigger hit than *Anarkali*.

Ajay Brahmatmaj says, 'What Pradeep Kumar is remembered even today for, is that the songs in his films always become very popular. How good an actor he was is a different matter, but the fact is that he was a handsome man who looked good on-screen. He was garnering recognition and had become a USP for Filmistan.'

Rono Mukerji tells us that the film was a flop for the first three weeks that it ran in Liberty Cinema hall. 'At that time Mehboob and Shantaram studios were partners in Liberty Cinema. S. Mukerji wanted to take the film off the theatres, declaring it a flop. Tolaram Jalan was the owner at that time, but he used to take Mukerji's advice. On that occassion though he said a firm no. And after those three weeks, *Nagin* became a bumper hit.'

What made *Nagin* memorable was its music—that tune by snake charmers which still rings in every corner of India.

Amit Khanna reveals, 'People actually believed for quite a few years that if you play the charmer's flute, snakes would come out crawling. And the instrument which was used in the film was not even a flute. It was a clavioline which Kalyanji used to play.'

After making stars out of Pradeep Kumar and Dilip Kumar, Filmistan added a new name to the Hindi film industry with *Nagin*. The famous actress of Tamil cinema—Vyjayanthimala—entered the industry through *Nagin*.

According to Tanishaa Mukerji, 'The era of dancing heroines started from there and it brought about a new aspect to the leading actress. If you see Madhuri Dixit, she also became so successful because she can dance so beautifully. So, that was something introduced with Vyjayanthimala and that Indian audience really connected with. It was a different way of portraying a heroine.'

Success had now become a regular feature of Filmistan, but the studio reached the pinnacle of success in 1954. That was not just a golden year for Filmistan but was also very unique for Hindi film industry because three films of the same studio, Filmistan, were amongst the top five highest grossing films of that year—*Nagin*, *Nastik* and *Jagriti*.

It is interesting to note that just like *Boot Polish*, which released in 1954, *Jagriti* too had a message for the children of the country which came forth in the songs of the poet, Kavi Pradeep.

Ajay Brahmatmaj says, 'It must have been on Pradeep's mind that the country is new, its dreams are fresh, which can be taken forward by its children, especially those born after independence or those who were growing up during those years. So, somewhere he tried to bring forth the dreams, aspirations and the imagination of the children.'

Jagriti was definitely a social-oriented film, but once again the times were changing and like any good producer Shashadhar Mukerji too understood the change in the direction of the winds. A new generation had grown up by then in Independent India and wanted a different kind of entertainment and, thus, in the times to come the language of cinema was about to witness a sea change.

By 1954, the grip of urban-themed films could be seen getting tighter on Hindi cinema. Filmistan was a commercial studio and the very next year they produced *Munimji* which was an out-an-out urban film, unlike its precedents.

Amit Khanna gives credit to S. Mukerji, 'When a new generation of directors came up to him—Nasir Hussain, Subodh Mukerji, etc.—they were contemporary people, out there to change the trend, and he encouraged them completely. This was very important that he was not crushed under the league. He was a progressive man.'

Munimji marked the debut of Shashadhar Mukerji's

younger brother Subodh Mukerji, as a director, who used the image of the urban star of that time, Dev Anand, in his story. Subodh Mukerji had learnt all the tactics of cinema while assisting at Filmistan. Hence, his very first film turned out to be a hit.

The trio of Subodh Mukerji, Nasir Hussain and Dev Anand continued its successful streak with Filmistan's next film, *Paying Guest*, in 1957.

Amrit Gangar explains, 'Our ancestors had no idea who a paying guest was. It was a time when people were migrating from villages to cities and scouting for places to live there. Just to choose this theme, was a reflection of the changing times.'

It can be said that the duo of Subodh Mukerji and Nasir Hussain laid the foundation of a new kind of cinema which some people label as the 'escapist cinema'. These films neither reflected patriotism nor socialism. What they were abundant in, was entertainment and a new formula. Today such films are called commercial films, which have a flavour of humour along with everything else needed to entertain an audience.

Ajay Brahmatmaj says, 'It was a time when commercial and art cinema were not divided. It began with Shashadhar Mukerji's films, or to be specific, the genres were separated by Nasir Hussain along with Subhodh Mukerji—which Hussain developed into an even bigger genre and later, Manmohan Desai fully established as "commercial cinema". This is where the roots of Hindi commercial cinema lie.'

Genre was new, the stories were new but there was

something else too that was fresh in the films of Filmistan—the hero's voice. Until then, in Hindi cinema the popular playback singers were Mohammad Rafi, Mukesh and Hemant Kumar. But to the new-age songs the voice that was lent to the male actors was of Kishore Kumar.

'Back then, he had decided to limit his voice either to the movies he acted in or playback only for Dev Anand,' Amit Kumar (Kishore Kumar's son) told Rajiv Vijayakar. Kishore Kumar and Dev Anand had become close friends during the making of *Ziddi* which was Dev Anand's major film and Kishore Kumar's first film as a playback singer.

After the success of *Paying Guest*, Subodh Mukerji got busy establishing his own production company, but Filmistan continued making escapist cinema. And another visionary became a part of Filmistan.

Born on 15 May 1931, Nasir Hussain had begun his career with Filmistan itself. He became a part of Filmistan in 1948, and after scriptwriting many hit films—he directed his first film *Tumsa Nahi Dekha* with the studio.

Rono Mukerji gives us the inside story, 'Tolaram Jalan had asked Subodh Mukerji to direct *Tumsa Nahi Dekha*. But Subhodh Mukerji wanted to give Nasir Hussain a break, so he kept a proposal before Tolaram Jalan—if he did not like the film, Subodh Mukerji would take the whole debt upon himself.' *Tumsa Nahi Dekha* went on to become a hit.

Tolaram Jalan wanted *Tumsa Nahi Dekha* to make a star out of the upcoming actress Ameetaa, but destiny had other plans. Meanwhile, after Dev Anand refused to work in this film, it went to—Shamsher Raj Kapoor, whom we know as Shammi Kapoor.

According to Ajay Brahmatmaj, 'Shammi Kapoor came at a time when the empire was being ruled by Dilip Kumar, Raj Kapoor and Dev Anand—yet he found acceptance in the audience. After a few flops, he found his feet in the film industry as a hero—the kind who was carefree, happy-go-lucky and didn't mind flirting with girls.'

Breaking out of the fixed acting styles of the three stars of the time, Shammi Kapoor built a whole new grammar of acting and a big attraction to his performance was his unique dancing style.

Tanishaa Mukerji tells us, 'Dada had told Shammi Kapoor to create his own personal style. After watching Elvis Presley, Shammi Kapoor decided to pick the rock and roll star's style itself. Dad was the kind of producer who took a leap of faith and gave him the freedom to display himself as crazy, mad, rough—all the charms of Elvis Presley—in his films.'

For this new star's new dancing style, a different kind of music was required. Filmistan chose O.P. Nayyar to compose that music, instead of their old favourite S.D. Burman, because Nayyar's music matched with the new Shammi Kapoor style more.

Rajiv Vijayakar tells us, 'O.P. Nayyar would make such songs that Shammi Kapoor would start dancing to them on hearing them only once, even if the film's production was yet to begin or the shoot was yet to start. Kapoor was a rebel when he danced to those songs, in the sense that he would touch the heroine and even hold her during its sequences—something that wan't even heard of back in the day.'

Tumsa Nahi Dekha may have given Shammi Kapoor a platform, but it also marks a change in the destiny of Filmistan yet again. It was the studio's last hit film.

After *Tumsa Nahi Dekha*, history repeated itself. Tolaram Jalan began to feel that he had understood the film business by then and did not need Shashadhar Mukerji anymore. Therefore, Shashadhar Mukerji decided to leave Filmistan.

According to Ajay Brahmatmaj, 'After the differences sprouted between the two, Shashadhar Mukerji left the studio. Even after his exit, some films came to the studio to be made probably due to Mukerji's reputation and residues. Those films gave Jalan a confidence because they did decent business. But on an independent level, he must have brought a few films on board too—and those didn't perform well. Eventually, things got so bad that the audience completely stopped paying attention to the films made under the banner of Filmistan.'

It is said that in those days the audience had become aware enough to judge films by its production house. They would expect certain things from a film depending on the studio that had made it. Their attention was not solely concentrated on the director, producer, or the actors. So, things degenerated to a point where people stopped watching the films by Filmistan.

Shashadhar Mukerji continued his journey in films with the successful team of *Tumsa Nahi Dekha* under a new production house called Filmalaya.

Rono Mukerji says, 'After the success of *Sargam*, S. Mukerji expected Tolaram Jalan to give a bonus to everyone. But Jalan did not do so. Things escalated quickly from there, as all the technicians of the studio would go to S. Mukerji and complain about Jalan. Thus, S. Mukerji left Filmistan and established a new studio, Fimalaya, for his people.'

From 1943–58, in fifteen years, Filmistan made twenty-seven films under Shashadhar Mukerji, out of which eighteen were box office hits. In the 40s and 50s, while the ropes of most of the studios were in the hands of actors, Filmistan was alone one such studio whose reins were handled by its producer.

Tanishaa Mukerji explains, 'He did not just make the studio, he also made stars.' She says that it is relevant in even today's age—the fact that S. Mukerji established back in the day that you don't have to be only an actor or director in order to make films. You only have to have passion. If you have zeal within you that you can make a film then you can make one for sure.

When we talk about successful films, we only think of the actors in those films. We give the credit of making a hit film only to its stars. But Filmistan showed us that behind good films there stands a talented coordinator who understands the nuances of filmmaking. Shashadhar Mukerji was one such man who made Filmistan a very successful studio and gave memorable films and stars to the Indian audience. And the name Filmistan is still very much a part of the history of Indian cinema.

FILMOGRAPHY

Chal Chal Re Naujawan (1944)
Mazdoor (1945)
Eight Days (1946)
Shikari (1946)
Do Bhai (1947)
Nadiya Ke Paar (1948)
Shaheed (1948)
Shabnam (1949)
Sargam (1950)
Shabistan (1951)
Anand Math (1952)
Anarkali (1953)
Jagriti (1954)
Nagin (1954)
Nastik (1954)
Shart (1954)
Aab-e-Hayat (1955)
Bhagwat Mahima (1955)
Munimji (1955)
Durgesh Nandini (1956)
Ham Sab Chor Hain (1956)
Heer (1956)

Champakali (1957)
Paying Guest (1957)
Tumsa Nahin Dekha (1957)
Sanskar (1958)
Khoobsurat Dhokha (1959)
Maine Jeena Seekh Liya (1959)
Babar (1960)
Dooj Ka Chand (1964)

6
MEHBOOB STUDIO
Cinema at its Grandest

Founder: Mehboob Khan (1907–64)

A journey of twenty-one years—from 1943 to 1964—of unparalleled films.

One Oscar nomination and two Filmfare Awards for Best Film and Best Director.

With strong female characters, every film was a social and political mirror of that time.

Six shooting floors and state-of-art sound studio.

Located in Bandra, Mumbai, their most iconic film was *Mother India*.

On every list of 'Best Films in Indian Cinema' one will always find the mention of *Mother India*.

Made on a budget of ₹40 lakh in 1957, *Mother India* was the most expensive film of its time. It was the first Indian film to be nominated for an Oscar, although it lost to *The Nights of Cabiria* by just one vote, under the Best Foreign Language Film category in 1958.

When discussing a film, the first thing that comes to mind are its actors. However, the mention of *Mother India* brings to memory not just the Hindi film stars Nargis, Rajkumar, Rajendra Kumar and Sunil Dutt, but also its director and producer, Mehboob Khan.

Mehboob Khan established the Mehboob Studio in 1943 and with the release of *Mother India* in 1957, the production house reached the pinnacle of its success. In these fourteen years, Mehboob Studio produced eleven films.

Mehboob Khan's journey started from Bilimora in Gujarat. When he came to Mumbai, he began working in the stable of Noor Mohammad Ali who used to provide horses for shooting.

Film producer Amit Khanna tells us how Khan began working in films, 'Chandrashekhar, a director from South, had hired a few horses and so Mehboob Khan had gone to his film set with those. He would be mostly sitting idle on the set because the scenes where horses were required were few and far in between. Because he didn't have much else to do, Khan began helping around on the set, without anybody having asked him to.'

About three years later, Mehboob Khan started working

as an extra in Ardeshir Irani's Imperial Film Company and in 1935 at the age of twenty-eight he directed his first film for Sagar Movitone, *Al Hilal*. In *Film India* magazine, after *Al Hilal*'s release, Baburao Patel had written for Mehboob Khan—'he will go far'.

Once Mehboob Khan became a director, he dabbled with different genres in a short span of time. In 1936, he made an action film called *Deccan Queen*, and after that he made a romantic drama, *Manmohan*, inspired by P.C. Barua's *Devdas*. In 1937 came the Hitchcockian mystery, *Jagirdar*. All these films were successful at the box office. But it was the 1938 film, *Hum Tum Aur Woh*, which placed Mehboob Khan's name in the league of the most famous film directors of all time. The film's story was of a woman who rebels against the society's norms for her wishes.

Amit Khanna explains Mehboob Khan's forethinking in *Hum Tum Aur Woh*, 'The 20s mark the first chapter of feminism, which went forward into the 30s. It is to Mehboob Khan's credit that he recognized this subtle change in the society that was happening and imbibed it in his films.'

While *Hum Tum Aur Woh* was the story of a helpless urban woman's rebellion, Mehboob Khan's next, *Aurat*, was the story of a single mother's struggle in a village. *Aurat* was inspired from Pearl S. Buck's novels—*The Good Earth* and *Mother*. Foreign films and literature had a deep impact on Mehboob Khan and it was usually visible in his stories.

K.A. Abbas had once called Mehboob Khan, 'A great

rustic'. Born and brought up in a small village, Mehboob Khan had great insight into the life in villages, the customs and norms, the aroma of the soil of villages and the people living there—and all of this almost came alive in *Aurat*.

Elaborating on Mehboob Khan's expertise in the genre, filmmaker Vinay Shukla says, 'One can see his attachment to villages through his films, so as to say, most of his films were rooted in villages. That is why all the drama in them: Mehboob Khan's drama was raw, there was no restraint in it. But it wasn't melodrama either. Our Asian culture is such that we are a little loud, our gestures are loud. He presented it all with such finesse and honesty that we could relate to its feeling that yes, it's our country, our soil.'

After *Aurat* and *Hum Tum Aur Woh*, in 1940 Mehboob Khan made the fantasy film, *Alibaba*. Based on *Arabian Nights*, the film was made in two languages—Hindi and Punjabi. Khan later married the film's heroine, Sardar Akhtar.

After the fantasy film *Alibaba*, Mehboob Khan once again turned towards a female-oriented film and in 1941 made *Behan*, which was the story of a girl who has been brought up by her elder brother, but when she grows up he does not want her to get married for fear of losing her. It was a very complex subject, not just then but even today.

Amit Khanna shares his opinion on the subject for *Behan*, 'There is a Freudian concept behind it. During the phase of pre-existentialism, such subjects were being mentioned in literature by writers like [Friedrich] Nietzsche and [André] Gide. One can argue that in a way *Behan* was almost an incestuous story, though there was no such scene. But the story inclined the delicate relationship to almost an edge.'

Aurat, *Behan* and *Hum Tum Aur Woh* proved that Mehboob Khan had an in-depth knowledge about the social issues of that time and to this dimension was added his next film, *Roti* (1942).

Every artiste's work is influenced by the circumstances he is surrounded with. In 1942, during World War II, many countries were moving towards capitalism and its consequences were visible in India too. It was during that time that Mehboob Khan made *Roti*, which took a dig at capitalism.

Screenwriter Anjum Rajabali explains why filmmakers of that time made social statements through their films, 'When an artiste develops a sensitive side towards the lesser privileged, then his position by default becomes that of a Leftist. Whether it is Guru Dutt or Bimal Roy or Mehboob Khan...they naturally became Leftists because they believed in equality, justice and made films on people who were deprived and underprivileged. Through their films they showed that in the same society where there are love stories and people living happy lives, there are also many others who are suffering and that it is important to tell their stories. Mehboob Khan's vision, as a filmmaker, always went in that direction.'

The interesting thing about *Roti* was the famous Kathak

dancer Sitara Devi playing the lead role and the playback was done by the queen of ghazal, Begum Akhtar.

Roti was Mehboob Khan's last film made for an outside studio. In the 40s when famous studios like Bombay Talkies and Calcutta's New Theatres were facing their decline, Mehboob Khan took the leap of faith and established his own studio in 1943—Mehboob Studio. And the team he'd selected for his production house made his social and political ideologies even more apparent.

Further elaborating on Khan's political stand, Amit Khanna says, 'In some way, he was influenced by Marxism. Inspired by communist ideologies, the logo of Mehboob Productions had a hammer and a sickle in it. It is accompanied by a voiceover which is a very famous couplet: *Muddayi lakh bura chahe toh kya hota hai, vahi hota hai jo manzoor-e-khuda hota hai.* Mehboob Khan was a strangely contradictory man. He was not a very orthodox Muslim but he was very proud of his faith.'

Till now the films that were being made in British India comprised of Hindu characters only. Mehboob Khan was the first director to break this tradition when in 1943 he made India's first Muslim social, *Najma*. In the future, *Najma* worked as a blueprint for all Muslim socials.

Najma was the first film produced by Mehboob Studio. 'A Muslim social is a genre in films that shows the Muslim culture and what all happens in a Muslim society. Back then, it had massive viewership. There was an audience who would look forward to such films because very few were making them. After the success of some of Mehboob Khan's films in this genre, many others also tried their hand at it,' explains journalist and author Rauf Ahmed.

In 1943, Bombay Talkies' film *Kismet* had made Ashok Kumar the country's biggest star. When Mehboob Productions offered Ashok Kumar ₹1 lakh for *Najma*, it set a record. The film went on to become such a success that for the next 20–25 years Ashok Kumar was the favourite choice for all Muslim socials.

After a successful film, the producer and director tend to stick to only big stars as they are more recognizable by the audience. But for his next film, *Taqdeer*, Mehboob Khan chose an upcoming actress—Fatima Rashid, better known as Nargis. It was her debut film as a lead actress and it placed her straight in the league of the popular mainstream heroines.

'Nargis had been a child star for years, but it was Mehboob Khan who saw a heroine's potential in her and cast her opposite Motilal. It was a big break for her at that time. And then they discovered that she could one day become a big star. Earlier she was known as Baby Fatima, but on becoming a lead actress she changed her name to Nargis,' says Rauf Ahmed.

After giving the film industry a new star, in 1946 Mehboob Productions was going to write a new history. A star cast which is considered the biggest casting coup of that time—Surendra, Suraiya and Noor Jahan—all three popular singing sensations brought together on-screen by

Mehboob Khan in *Anmol Ghadi*.

'His films were very successful on the box office. That was why the big stars used to agree to work with him. Therefore, when he made *Anmol Ghadi* all the three big stars were interested in the plot and but had this condition that Mehboob would give them all equal importance,' says Amit Khanna.

Anmol Ghadi proved to be the biggest hit of 1946 in which the film's music contributed in a big way. This film marked the start of the collaboration between music composer Naushad and Mehboob Productions which continued till their last film, *Son of India*.

Mehboob Khan had proved one thing with his films that he was not limited to any genre. But there was one binding thread through all his films that apart from entertaining the audience there must always be a message for the society in them. In the year of India's independence, Mehboob Productions released the film *Elan*. That film raised questions about the Muslim society's rites and rituals and also the Quranic reforms. It's a controversial theme, that too in 1947, the film was banned for some time.

Rauf Ahmed elaborates on Mehboob Khan's personality, 'Though he was conservative in many ways, he was also progressive in his thinking. He didn't show it much, but a part of him always believed that there was a conflict in the Indian society regarding the Muslims being a part of it and yet living their lives separately in many ways, such as the purdah system. He did feel this segregation.'

By now Mehboob Productions had made four films and they were all hits at the box office. Mehboob Khan himself came to be known as a hit film director, and he further proved his mettle by making a multi-starrer with the three biggest stars of the time. In 1949, came *Andaz* starring Nargis, Raj Kapoor and Dilip Kumar—the one and only film in which the three of them have worked together.

Whether it was a love triangle, a fantasy or a political film, the female characters in all Mehboob Khan films have been complex. In *Andaz*, Nargis's character was complex as well as bold. It was about a girl who fails to understand why she cannot keep her relationship with an old friend after her marriage.

'Mehboob Sahab and S. Ali Raza Sahab, who had written it, were asked why the film concluded in a tragedy: a man dies, the heroine goes to jail, her daughter becomes an orphan, Raj Kapoor is left alone, why did it all happen? Their response was that it all happened because the woman in the story was not behaving as a Hindustani lady should behave. She was behaving in a free Western way because of which all the misunderstanding happened. Now, conceptually it was a modern outlook but when the conclusion comes, we are shown that actually it was the girl's fault. This was a departure from generally speaking (how) Mehboob Khan treated his women,' says film writer Anjum Rajabali.

Upon its release, *Andaz* became the highest grossing

film until then. Then three years later, in 1952, Mehboob Productions made India's first technicolour film—*Aan*.

After the success of *Andaz*, *Aan* was Mehboob Khan's second successive film with Dilip Kumar. It was also actress Nadira's debut film. *Aan* was the first Indian film which got a worldwide release and its premiere happened in London. Made on a budget of ₹35 lakh, it did a business of ₹1.5 crore and proved to be the biggest hit of that time.

'*Aan* was clearly inspired from Hollywood. It showed Dilip Kumar swashbuckling where he would just pull out his sword and start fighting, and even the female protagonist who was a princess, the setting of the film, the palaces shown—it looked like Mehboob Khan had made a film to show to the audience of the entire world,' feels journalist and writer Sidharth Bhatia.

Mehboob Khan had directed twenty films so far and the last eight of those he had produced himself. Mehboob Productions had now become a successful brand and in 1953 came out with its next film, *Amar*. It was a psychological drama and the studio's third film with Dilip Kumar. Although *Amar* was not very successful at the box office but Mehboob Khan considered this film the closest to his heart. It had Dilip Kumar playing a young lawyer, in love with Madhubala, but rapes a local village girl.

Sidharth Bhatia explains us the reason behind *Amar*'s failure, 'The audience found it difficult to accept Dilip Kumar as a hero who was a rapist. Although rape is suggested in a very discrete and nuanced manner. It can even be called seduction; the hero actually seduces that village belle by grabbing her. But it was unacceptable to the Indian viewers. That's the norm in Hindi films, a rapist will always be the bad guy and nothing else. Even in today's times, it is unlikely that any film will ever portray a rapist as its hero.'

Despite making so many successful films and believing *Amar* to be its best work, the most iconic movie of Mehboob Productions was yet to come.

When a filmmaker wants to remake a film of his own from years ago, it's most likely because he could not express himself fully the last time. Mehboob Khan's best work came in 1957—*Mother India*. It was inspired from his own film, *Aurat*, which he had made seventeen years ago.

Amit Khanna, elaborates on the importance of *Mother India*, 'If we look at the history of Indian cinema, in the last hundred years probably just about 12–15 films have permanently imprinted on people's memories and stood the test of time, such as—*Mother India, Ganga Jamuna, Mughal-e-Aazam, Sholay*, among others. These films became the landmarks or the milestones because even today they are cinematically and thematically valid.'

Katherine Mayo, an American writer, wrote a book insulting Indian women and its society in 1927. The book's title was *Mother India*. Mehboob Khan chose exactly that title for his iconic film because he meant it as a response to that book.

Anjum Rajabali explains the film's theme, 'For *Mother India*, Mehboob Khan expanded the canvas so much so that the story of Radha, the protagonist, became a metaphor for India. His view was that the kind of challenges that Radha was facing was the same kind the country was trying to overcome at that point of time. The film showed Radha getting married and dreaming of a happy, secure, dignified and respectful life. But then suddenly her husband Shamu dies and Radha's life becomes ridden with troubles. The same was with India, we had so many dreams after Independence but to materialize those it took a lot of struggle. The moral was that if you hold on to your basic values and try to do the right thing, you will still have to pay the price and make a lot of sacrifices.'

Mehboob Khan had already made three films with Nargis prior to *Mother India*. She was one of the biggest stars of the time, but was mostly seen playing urban characters. But in *Mother India*, she played the role of an illiterate village belle Radha and it went on to become her career defining role. She got the 1957 Filmfare Award for Best Actress for it.

Elaborating on Nargis, Rauf Ahmed tells us, 'She was beginning to get frustrated with the kind of roles she was doing. She wanted to do a film where she could prove her acting mettle, a film that would immortalize her in the memory of the audience. This frustration was at its peak after Shambhu Mitra's film *Jagte Raho*, in which he cast her opposite Raj Kapoor. And she knew that Raj Kapoor would never let her have what she wanted, he would always see to it that he had the most important part in every film. So, she quietly discussed her feelings with Mehboob Khan and when Raj Kapoor came to know of it, he was really shattered.'

By mid-50s, the producers and directors had realized that music was a major attraction to pull the audience to the theatres. When legendary music director Naushad started working on the music of *Mother India*, for the next one year he did not sign any other film.

Mother India was India's first film which got nominated under the Best Foreign Language Film category in the Oscars, and Nargis was the first Indian actress to be honoured with the Best Actress Award at the Karlovy Vary International Film festival. *Mother India* got honoured with the Filmfare Awards for the Best Film, Best Director, Best Actress, Best Cinematography and Best Sound. Many film historians believe that *Mother India* is the Indian equivalent to Hollywood's *Gone with the Wind*.

'*Mother India* put India on the map of the celluloid world. Unlike the other smaller films, this one symbolized India and the most important thing is that the theme reflected India and the international audience was immediately struck by the Indian-ness of the film,' says Rauf Ahmed.

There are many interesting stories associated with *Mother India* but the most interesting one is of Nargis and Sunil Dutt who played the mother and son in the film. During the shooting of the film, Sunil Dutt had saved Nargis from a fire that had broken out on the set, getting himself a little hurt in the process. The accident helped develop affection between the two of them, leading to love and eventually marriage.

After the success of *Mother India* everyone was awaiting the next film of Mehboob Productions. It was *Son of India*, which came in 1962 and flopped at the box office. The biggest flop of Mehboob Productions was the last film of Mehboob Khan.

India lost two of its stalwarts in 1964, one from politics and the other from the world of cinema. A day after the death of Jawaharlal Nehru, on 28 May 1964, at the age of just 57, Mehboob Khan too passed away.

Amit Khanna says, 'He had been unwell for some time and then he suffered a heart attack. Some of his close friends say that Nehru's death was a shock to him. He had not been well, and when he heard the news the very next day he died.'

After the demise of Mehboob Khan and particularly after the failure of *Son of India*, the financial burden on Mehboob Productions increased. Although several films by other directors were shot in Mehboob Studio but there was no one to steer Mehboob Productions forward.

'He had three sons but none of them was a filmmaker; it is not necessary that a filmmaker's son or daughter will be a filmmaker too. But it's commendable that Mehboob Studio still stands tall today and films are shot there. It has its place secured that way, but yes, as a film production company it did not prosper further,' says Amit Khanna.

Mehboob Khan directed twenty-six films, of which twenty were successful at the box office. His films are not just remembered for big stars, big budgets and big sets but also for his social views and his portrayal of the class conflicts. The Government of India honoured him with the title of Hidayatkar-e-Azam and in 2007, at a function held at Mehboob Studio, Indian Postal Service launched a postal stamp in the memory and honour of Mehboob Khan.

Amit Khanna believes, 'Mehboob Khan was India's first complete filmmaker, along with V. Shantaram. He could make magnificent spectacles, taking a wide canvas he could handle big productions. Firstly, because he had a broad vision and his films raised authentic issues in the Indian society. And secondly, because of the dramatic effects he had in his films—*unbelievable*! Even if you watch his films today, you'll learn something from them.'

Fifty years have passed since Mehboob Khan's demise, but even today his name is there in the minds of every person associated with cinema. *Anmol Ghadi*, *Aan*, *Andaz*, *Mother India* and Bandra-based Mehboob Studio will always be associated with the history as well as the future of Indian films.

FILMOGRAPHY

Al Hilal (1935)
Deccan Queen (1936)
Manmohan (1936)
Alibaba (1940)

Aurat (1940)
Bahen (1941)
Najma (1943)
Taqdeer (1943)
Humayun (1945)
Anmol Ghadi (1946)
Elan (1947)
Anokhi Ada (1948)
Andaz (1949)
Aan (1953)
Amar (1953)
Jhansi Ki Rani (1956)
Aawaz (1956)
Mother India (1957)
A Handful of Grain (1959)
Son of India (1962)

7

RAJSHRI PRODUCTIONS
Family Entertainer

Founder: Tarachand Barjatya (1914–92)

Twenty-four box office hits in fifty-three years.

Six National Awards and twenty-seven Filmfare Awards.

Known for traditional family entertainment.

Gave breaks to Salman Khan, Madhuri Dixit and Anupam Kher.

The makers of blockbusters like *Maine Pyaar Kiya* and *Hum Aapke Hain Koun..!*

Rajshri Productions' latest film *Prem Ratan Dhan Payo*, their fourth venture with actor Salman Khan, was released on 12 November 2015. Its director Sooraj

Barjatya once again chose the same subject for which Rajshri Productions is known: family values, family relations and the disagreements within families. But it also had the special touch of Sooraj Barjatya—magnanimous sets, popular music and larger-than-life picturization. This film did a business of more than ₹200 crore at the box office.

Since 1962, Rajshri Productions has been a name associated with the Indian culture and clean entertainment. Every character, in its films, is valued on the scale of relationships and the hallmark of each film has always been its hit music.

The founder of Rajshri Productions, Tarachand Barjatya, was born on 10 May 1914 in Rajasthan. After completing his education from Vidyasagar College, Kolkata, he started working in Moti Mahal Theatres in 1933, which was a film distribution company in Kolkata. After fourteen years of experience in the distribution business, he decided to open his own company. On 15 August 1947, with the beginning of a new country, began Rajshri Pictures in Mumbai and so began the journey of his dreams.

Journalist Jyothi Venkatesh reveals that people used to call Tarachand Barjatya, 'Sethji'. 'Sethji had become an expert after distributing films in Rawalpindi, Karachi and many other cities. He used to work as the General Manager of Moti Mahal Theatres, earlier. Later, the owner of Moti Mahal was so impressed by him that he financed Sethji's company, Rajshri Pictures in 1947.'

Within fifteen years, the distribution offices of Rajshri Pictures were in every corner of the country and it became the only 'All-India' film distribution company. Encouraged with this success, Tarachand Barjatya put his next foot forward and in 1962 established Rajshri Productions. The first film made under the banner of Rajshri Productions was *Aarti*. The actors in it were Ashok Kumar, Meena Kumari, Pradeep Kumar and Shashikala. *Aarti* was a hit at the box office.

Jyothi Venkatesh futher tells us that Tarachand Barjatya had always said to him that he was in the business to do business, 'He had no inclination of making art films and he did not feel that filmmaking was an art, but strictly a business. With *Aarti*, he earned a lot as a distributer. He felt that he could fully venture into both distribution and production. He also had the exhibition outlets to him—he wanted to be a producer, exhibitor and distributer.'

The 1960s were ruled by Shammi Kapoor and Dev Anand's flamboyance and romance. But Tarachand Barjatya was brought up in a joint family and that reflected in his films which had themes like familial tension and its impact on relationships. Eventually, this became the hallmark of Rajshri films.

After the success of its first film *Aarti*, Rajshri Productions chose an unconventional subject for their second film. In 1964 came *Dosti*, directed by Satyam Bose. It was the story of the struggle of two handicapped friends: one blind and the other a cripple. The two characters were shown never letting go of goodness and humanity, irrespective of the insurmountable difficulties. *Dosti* went on to become the third biggest hit of 1964 and won six Filmfare Awards including the one for Best Film.

Grandson of Tarachand Barjatya, the late Rajjat A. Barjatya, former MD and CEO of Rajshri Media Pvt. Ltd. had once said that the film that had established them in the true sense was *Dosti*—a wonderful, heart-wrenching story of true love and friendship. He had said, 'It was *Dosti* which brought Rajshri to the forefront as a film production banner, one that made films on its own terms and was not dictated by market forces.'

Made with two debutants, *Dosti* was had a sensitive subject. A big contributor to its success was the film's music composed by Laxmikant-Pyarelal, for which the duo also won their first Filmfare Award. Here's an interesting trivia about *Dosti*'s music—the mouth organ for it was actually played by R.D. Burman.

Music historian Rajiv Vijayakar reminisces, 'When Rajshri's first production, *Aarti*, became a success on a grand level, its music by Roshan Sahab had also become a hit. So, he was expected to compose music for their next film too. But when Roshan Sahab heard the film's story, he wondered what music he could possibly give to a story of two beggars. At the same time, Laxmikant-Pyarelal were arranging the music for many dubbed films which Tarachand Barjatya was distributing. He spotted the duo and the rest is history.'

By the 70s, films were being made with big budgets and big star casts and escapist cinema had become the major mantra of Bollywood. But Rajshri Productions' emphasis remained on social and human relationships. In 1971, while on the one hand there were films like *Caravan* and *Haré*

Rama Haré Krishna being made, on the other hand Rajshri Productions made a film on Rabindranath Tagore's short story 'Samapti' called *Uphaar*, which was the story of a girl who after her marriage did not want to lose the innocence of her childhood.

Shyam Shroff, MD of Shringar Films Pvt. Ltd., elaborates on Rajshri's films, 'Tarachand Barjatya's films were known for their storylines, but also the values that he incorporated in them which is what attracted families to it. So, at a time when most films showed villains, violence and crimes, he brought in clean films with good stories, music, talented actors and directors. That credit goes to him.'

Along with its storylines, Rajshri Productions also made unconventional casting choices in its films. In 1973, besides playing an urban hero in films like *Abhimaan*, *Namak Haram* and *Zanjeer*, Amitabh Bachchan also played the non-glamorous role in Rajshri Production's *Saudagar*. Although the music of the film was a success but the film was not a hit at the box office. Despite the failure of *Saudagar*, Rajshri continued with its belief in stories related to traditions. In the year 1975, amongst big films like *Sholay* and *Deewar*, came Rajshri's *Geet Gaata Chal*. This film had former child stars Sachin Pilgaonkar and Sarika in lead roles. The story, once again, was about love and sacrifice.

Sachin Pilgaonkar recalls meeting Tarachand Barjatya for the film, 'Sethji had seen a Marathi film of mine, for which I had won the National Award, and wanted to see me in his office. When I went there, Sethji told me that Rajshri wants to make a film with me in which I would play the hero. But he also added that they didn't have a story for it yet, to which I expressed concern that it might take them a while to find a story. But Sethji was confident when he said that they would find the story soon and I should not worry, and that they wanted to make a film with me.'

The film was made and released, but there was no collection on Friday. Pilgaonkar continues, 'Saturday was better but not very encouraging. Sunday they were hoping that people would come, it being a holiday, but they didn't come. And on Monday, the first show went houseful and Tuesday was even better. On Wednesday, the theatre people themselves called and said that they would run the film for another week because people were coming and appreciating it. The following week, right from Friday onwards all shows were houseful.'

Like *Dosti*, the biggest reason behind the success of *Geet Gaata Chal* was its music which proved to be the most popular soundtrack of 1975. This film marked the beginning of a thirty-six-year-long association of Ravindra Jain and Rajshri.

Pilgaonkar shares an anecdote with us, 'Dadu [Ravindra Jain] was one of Sethji's pet music directors. He composed the song "*Geet Gaata Chal/O Saathi Gungunata Chal*" in front us and I got to enjoy the song while it was in process. It was after this song that Raj Babu at Rajshri decided that they would keep the name of the film *Geet Gaata Chal*.' The hero and heroine of the film in the true sense—are its music and lyrics respectively, and after that, Sachin and Sarika.

Rajshri was a successful production house now with eleven films and many Filmfare awards. Its next—*Tapasya* (1976)—got Rajshri its first National Award. *Tapasya* was the story of a woman who sacrifices her happiness and dreams for her brothers and sisters, but only receives their ungratefulness in return. It was based on a short story by the Bengali writer Ashapoorna Devi, and was directed by Anil Ganguly. 'Sethji believed that if women can be attracted through films, then automatically family and socially themed films can do good business and so, *Tapasya* was the beginning of his women-centric films,' avers Jyothi Venkatesh.

Tapasya's heroine was Rakhee who had made her Hindi debut with Rajshri's *Jeevan Mrityu* in 1970. By 1975, Rakhee was a star in Hindi films but in *Tapasya* her deglamourized and tragic character was in absolute contrast to her image. Rakhee got the Filmfare Best Actress Award that year for her role.

'Sethji had a conviction that the actor should suit the role, not the star suiting the role. When Anil Da [Ganguly] said that Rakhee can't play the character as she fits modern roles only, Sethji disagreed and insisted they take her and no one else. In those days, it was he who had started the trend of auditions and Rakhee was willing to accept the challenge. She gave the audition and succeeded in breaking through her screen image through that role,' states Venkatesh.

Although Rajshri Productions had become a household name by then, but the next five years proved to be their golden phase. Each film made by them was a hit, and this successful streak began with Basu Chatterjee's *Chitchor*.

By mid-70s Hindi cinema was divided between commercial and art films. During this period, Rajshri had carved its identity with a special kind of cinema—low budget family films, with characters that were beacons of sacrifice and love.

Rajjat A. Barjayta had said, 'My grandfather always used to tell me that "we should make films which we can watch with our family". And as filmmakers we have a huge responsibility towards society. So, a film can shape an entire generation. Why not shape them the right way? That's the responsibility that we have taken onto ourselves of providing clean, wholesome, family entertainment and influencing a generation in a positive manner.'

After making thirteen family-oriented films, in 1977 Rajshri Productions made *Agent Vinod*, with the newcomer Mahendra Sandhu. *Agent Vinod* was a spy thriller made on the lines of the James Bond films. This was the first time that a film was made by the studio that was away from its favourite genre.

Venkatesh recounts Tarachand Barjatya's response when he asked the latter that why did he shift from his favourite genre and made *Agent Vinod*. 'He told me that earlier he was the lone decision-maker. But that was no more the case.

His sons had grown up and they too brought ideas to the table. It was their take that their films should change with the changing times. They wanted to float multiple banners to make films of different genres under them. For instance, under the Rajshri banner there would be family and social films, but under Sargam Pictures they would experiment with themes. That's how *Agent Vinod* got made. As for the collections, *Agent Vinod* didn't do well. The audience also wondered that why did Rajshri make a film like that. So, they had to naturally stop experimenting further.'

In the 70s, Bollywood was under the grip of the star system. Every successful producer was trying to make films with the big stars. Tarachand Barjatya was an experienced distributer and could identify the vein of the market. In this era of films with star power, Rajshri Productions chose to make films with new actors like Prem Kishan, Rameshwari, Arun Govil, Mithun Chakraborty, Ranjeeta and Vijayendra Ghatge, and gave the utmost importance to content and music.

According to Shyam Shroff, 'If you have made a good film and you know there is no star cast in it but you yourself are confident that the film is brilliant and can do business, the audience come on its own. But Tarachand Barjatya also knew that no audience will come to watch such films on the very first day. So, he started showcasing his films with very few prints in only a few places and then got them publicity slowly through word of mouth. But this strategy is only possible when you have full conviction in your own product, which he proved.'

As we entered a new decade in the 80s, the three sons of Tarachand Barjatya—Kamal Kumar, Raj Kumar and Ajit Kumar—were also a part of Rajshri Productions. Along with being a successful films producer, Rajshri Production's film distribution business had also been doing well. But, at this point things went a little downhill as amidst the ever-expanding budgets and glamour-filled films, Rajshri's simple films got lost somewhere. The studio had to wait a long time for their next hit.

'It was a time when new mediums like colour television, video, etc., were coming up. So, people felt that if they can sit at home and watch films then what is the need to go out? This had caused a gap of eight to ten years in the film industry when people did not step out of their houses to watch films. It even led to depletion in the quality of cinema theatres,' believes Shyam Shroff.

The only hit Rajshri had in this period was the film *Nadiya Ke Paar* that came in 1982. The USP of the film were its dialogues which were a mix of Avadhi and Bhojpuri dialects that are spoken in Bihar and eastern Uttar Pradesh. Despite failures, Rajshri Productions did not change its path and ideologies with success or failure. Probably this was the reason why my own (Mahesh Bhatt's) script, *Saraansh*, which several producers had refused, was agreed to be made by Rajshri Productions in 1984. Rajshri probably chose *Saraansh* because it had the same glimpse of relationships and humanity which was always seen in their films.

Actor Anupam Kher shares his experience of acting in *Saraansh*, 'When *Saraansh* began being made, I was very happy. A lot of people questioned why I was playing the role of a 65-year-old man when I was only 28 or 29 years old at the time. My answer was always that the role was great and had I not done that as my first film I probably would not have reached where I have and managed to be here for thirty-one years.' He adds that with Rajshri being its producer, the film got elevated to another level, 'It's very important that the producers believe in the film. So, speaking that way, they are the only production house in our country who have stuck to their principles of making a certain kind of cinema.'

In 1984, Rajshri Production gave two amazing artistes to Indian cinema—Anupam Kher who debuted in *Saraansh* and Madhuri Dixit in *Abodh*, who in later years became the most popular actress of her times.

Anupam Kher believes that the number of newcomers Rajshri Productions has introduced, no other production house has done so far. 'In the 80s especially, they never really worked with very big stars.'

Tarachand Barjatya was 70 years old now. His three sons were already handling the production and distribution work. Now was the turn of the third generation of the Barjatya family to also enter the business. His grandson, Sooraj Barjatya, was ready to direct his own film after having assisted me in *Saraansh*. But it took full five years for the next film of Rajshri Productions to release which was *Maine Pyaar Kiya* that came in 1989. The film proved to be the biggest blockbuster of that year. Sooraj Barjatya incorporated all the features of Rajshri Productions, like Indian culture, importance of family and good music in *Maine Pyaar Kiya*. But the packaging of the film was modern and the canvas larger than life, which later went on to become the trademark style of Sooraj Barjatya.

Jyothi Venkatesh recalls an interesting backstory to the blockbuster, 'Sooraj had to literally fight, though lovingly, with Sethji because the latter was of old values and Sooraj, a newcomer of the modern era. Sooraj said that he wants to bring something new starting from the title, and that he would bring modernity without vulgarity. Sooraj took in his hands everything including the choice of actors, so that a lot of new appeal could be brought to the film. The story was traditional at its core, yet Sooraj made it with a fresh appeal because of which it became an unprecedented success.' He adds that music certainly was a dominating factor in the film, 'S.P. Balasubrahmanyam was brought to playback for the debutant Salman Khan—Balasubrahmanyam was already an established and extreme popular singer from the South. The film's soundtrack had quite a bit of Western influence as the melodies of some its songs had been lifted from popular English songs on Sooraj's insistence. He was aware of what the youth was fond of and that they wouldn't be keen on Indian classical-based music. That's the reason why the songs of *Maine Pyaar Kiya* are still remembered.'

On 29 December 1989, *Maine Pyar Kiya* released with

just 29 prints. It was made on a budget of ₹2 crore and did a business of more that ₹24 crore, which in today's time would be approximately ₹80 crore—a total smashing hit. Though *Maine Pyar Kiya* did spectacular business, Rajshri's biggest hit film was yet to come. For five years after it, they did not make any film. Rajshri, which had always been known to give a break to new directors, did not sign a single director from outside or make any film. It was evident that only Sooraj Barjatya was going to direct the films for the studio.

Rajjat Barjatya had said that the family's vision had changed. They only wanted to make one film at a time and Sooraj Barjatya was able to fulfil that vision. He said, 'We never wanted to scale up and make twelve films in a year, the way studios are making today. Whether right or wrong, that was the vision of our family to make one film at a time and put everything into it and make it special.'

The year was 1994 and Sooraj Barjatya was ready with his next film, *Hum Aakpe Hain Koun..!* but unfortunately, Tarachand Barjatya did not live to see the biggest success of Rajshri Productions. In 1992, at the age of 78 he passed away but his legacy was taken forward by his grandson.

Hum Aapke Hain Koun..! was the remake of Rajshri Productions' own 1982 hit, *Nadiya Ke Paar*. It did a business of ₹70 crore which in today's time would be more than ₹350 crore. It also won five Filmfare Awards.

Sachin Pilgaonkar believes that the personality of a filmmaker definitely reflects in his work. 'So is the case at Rajshri Productions. They all like to sit together with the whole family to eat, and you must have noticed the same is shown in their films too. They eat vegetarian food but dastarkhwan (the spread) is so lavish that people feel hungry just seeing that. I remember that after watching *Hum Aapke Hain Koun..!* I had gone home and had sweets the first thing because they had fed such delicious sweets and laddoos in that film too', he says, adding that who wouldn't like to see a neat, clean, happy family on screen?

According to Anupam Kher, 'The traditional values of Sooraj Barjatya's films, like the kind of clothes worn, the kind of food served, the fun at the wedding (shown in the song "*Didi Tera Devar Deewana*" in *Hum Aapke Hain Koun..!*) became a very big point of reference to many big directors, like Aditya Chopra and Karan Johar, in future.' 'If you look at the wedding sequences in Karan Johar's films, the kind of clothes the actors wear and the fun and teasing shown during those are influenced by him [Sooraj]. He is the kind of person to whom you can easily say "I am your fan", without thinking that he is your contemporary actually', Kher adds.

The year was 1999. The century was going to change soon. The films that were being made then were mostly set in the metros and were youth-centric. Rajshri, however did not depart from its identity and made their next film inspired from the Ramayana. The film was *Hum Saath Saath Hain*.

Rajjat Barjatya had explained the concept behind it, 'In our case, it's very true because we are a joint family in the true sense of the term. We are sixteen of us who live together. It was my grandfather who founded the company and his three sons took it forward. It is an amazing feeling of being together, truly *Hum Saath Saath Hain* (we are all together).'

Hum Saath Saath Hain became one of the biggest hits of 1999 and Rajshri Productions established in 1962 stepped into the new century with it. Hindi cinema was developing a new vision in the new century. At this point, Rajshri Production casted two new actors of that time, Hrithik Roshan and Abhishek Bachchan, in *Main Prem Ki Diwani Hoon* which was a remake of their own 1976 hit, *Chitchor*. Instead of a traditional family, this film had a modern family, Valentine's Day celebrations instead of Diwali, 'Hi' instead of 'Namaste' and skirts instead of sarees. The story was like a traditional Rajshri film but this time the look and feel of the film was modern.

Venkatesh elaborates, 'Sooraj tried to break all the points that Rajshri had emphasized on over the years and for the first time there was a hint of vulgarity between the lead couple Hrithik and Kareena, which was not appreciated by the majority of the audience. *Main Prem Ki Diwani Hoon* was an attempt to do something different by Sooraj Barjatya. He wanted to break away from the conservative identity of Rajshri, but in the process of doing that and trying to make a modern film he got stuck and ended up reaching neither ends.'

However, Rajjat Barjatya had admitted that it happened because every director wants to evolve. 'Every studio wants to evolve. They understand the audience has evolved but you have to do so within the parameters of your values and your principles.' So, he believed that you cannot let go of your values and principles. 'That's the mistake that we made in *Main Prem Ki Diwani Hoon*,' he confessed.

After *Main Prem Ki Diwani Hoon* bombed at the box office, Rajshri Productions once again turned towards their tried-and-tested formula. Two years later, in 2006, released the next film of Rajshri Productions—*Vivaah*. The storyline once again revolved around middle-class values and moralities. With a business of ₹23 crore, *Vivaah* was the fifth biggest hit of that year.

Shyam Shroff adds that stories, like *Vivah* still work, 'It was probably inspired from *Tapasya*, their own production in 1976. That kind of a story, that kind of a family with a stepsister and stepmother, and made with a good (value) system...appeals to people even today.'

After the success of *Vivaah*, Rajshri adopted a new business model. They stepped into television serials and digital media, which was started by Sooraj Barjatya's brother Rajjat and sister Kavita. Along with it, the studio also started making films with directors outside the family, like *Ek Vivaah Aisa Bhi* (dir: Kaushik Ghatak; 2008), *Isi Life Mein...!* (dir: Vidhi Kasliwal; 2010), *Love u..Mr. Kalakar!* (dir: S. Manasi; 2011), *Jaane Pehchaane* (dir: Sachin Pilgaonkar; 2011) and *Samrat & Co.* (dir: Kaushik Ghatak; 2014).

This change happened as around mid-2000s when Rajshri started to see itself as an entertainment company, and not just a production company. Rajjat Barjatya had explained this change in vision, 'There are five screens in your life—cinema, television, computer, mobile phones and tablet computers which were just coming up that time. For us, these five screens are really entertainment screens. So we wondered if as Rajshri are we film producers or an entertainment company? We realized we are an entertainment company which really means that we had to produce content and entertain people across these five screens and not just cinema.'

They have produced a number of TV soaps, which include *Woh Rehne Waali Mehlon Ki, Yahaaan Main Ghar Ghar Kheli, Pyaar Ka Dard Hai Meetha Meetha Pyaara Pyaara, Mere Rang Mein Rangne Waali* and more recently, *Piyaa Albela*.

In November 2015, Rajshri Productions' *Prem Ratan Dhan Payo* released, which was directed by Sooraj Barjatya himself after a break of nine years. In this film too, the long-standing symbols of Rajshri tradition can be seen— clean and clear entertainment, drama woven with family relationships and the basic values of humanity. This is the biggest contribution of Rajshri Productions to cinema that even in changing times they kept Indian culture and tradition alive in their films.

Jyothi Venkatesh remarks that Rajshri Productions is the only A–Z production house. 'It is a film institution and a production house which did direction, exhibition and distribution. It gave innumerable newcomers to the industry who later became stars,' he maintains. Anupam Kher adds, 'If there is someone who has preserved the tradition, culture of our country and its values—it is Rajshri Productions.'

Even today the Barjatya family is together in both

personal and professional spheres like a big joint family. In film production, distribution, television, digital and music, now the third generation of Rajshri Production is successfully taking the company forward. It wouldn't be wrong to say that the *khwaboon ka safar* of Rajshri Productions has not ended yet.

FILMOGRAPHY

Aarti (1962)
Dosti (1964)
Taqdeer (1967)
Jeevan Mrityu (1970)
Uphaar (1971)
Piya Ka Ghar (1972)
Mere Bhaiya (1972)
Honeymoon (1973)
Saudagar (1973)
Toofan (1975)
Geet Gaata Chal (1975)
Tapasya (1976)
Chitchor (1976)
Agent Vinod (1977)
Dulhan Wahi Jo Piya Man Bhaaye (1977)
Alibaba Marjinaa (1977)
Paheli (1977)
Ankhiyon Ke Jharokhon Se (1978)
Shikshaa (1979)
Sunayana (1979)

Saanch Ko Aanch Nahin (1979)
Gopaal Krishna (1979)
Raadha Aur Seeta (1979)
Tarana (1979)
Sawan Ko Aane Do (1979)
Naiyya (1979)
Manokaamnaa (1980)
Maan Abhiman (1980)
Ek Baar Kaho (1980)
Humkadam (1980)
Payal Ki Jhankaar (1980)
Jazbaat (1980)
Jiyo To Aise Jiyo (1981)
Tumhaare Bina (1982)
Nadiya Ke Paar (1982)
Sun Sajna (1982)
Sun Meri Laila (1983)
Dard-E-Dil (1983)
Phulwari (1984)
Rakt Bandhan (1984)
Saaransh (1984)
Abodh (1984)
Rimjhim Geeton Ki (1985)
Babul (1986)
Maine Pyar Kiya (1989)
Hum Aapke Hain Koun..! (1994)
Hum Saath Saath Hain (1999)
Hum Pyar Tumhi Se Kar Baithe (2002)
Main Prem Ki Diwani Hoon (2003)

Uuf Kya Jadoo Mohabbat Hai..! (2004)
Vivah (2006)
Ek Vivaah... Aisa Bhi (2008)
Isi Life Mein...! (2010)
Love U...Mr. Kalakaar! (2011)
Jaana Pehchana (2011)
Samrat & Co. (2014)
Prem Ratan Dhan Payo (2015)

8
R.K. STUDIOS

First Independent Studio of Independent India

Founder: Raj Kapoor (1924-88)

Located in Chembur, Mumbai.

Spread over six acres of land.

In its journey of fifty-one years till 1999, the studio gave twenty-one unique films.

The studio identified with powerful social themes and love stories.

It received three National Awards in the Best Film category, three Filmfare Awards in the Best Film category and four in the Best Director category.

The first independent proprietorship studio of Independent India—R.K. Studios.

The story of R.K. Studio and the history of India have moved together in a parallel direction. In fact, in every decade our social circumstances were better visible in the films made by R.K. Studio than in the government surveys.

From the Nehruvian socialism of the 50s to the brain drain of the 90s; from a 'dehati' (simple village guy) to the 'suit-boot' clad thug; from trams to vamps; family feuds to evils of the society; and many more such matters concerning the country. We got to see all this and more in the films by R.K. Studio, infused with entertainment.

While 1947 marked the establishment of a new nation, 1948 marked the birth of Independent India's first independent sole proprietorship studio—R.K. Studios.

According to film historian Ashish Rajadhyaksha, the studio era had two phases, 'The first phase was what we call the joint stock companies which had partnerships, like Prabhat Studio which had five partners and a corporate structure. But in the early 1940s a new structure emerged when V. Shantaram left Prabhat and started Rajkamal Kalamandir and Raj Kapoor started R.K. Studios. It was more along the lines of proprietorships where you had single producers who often had financiers who were so to say the 'invisible men'. For instance, V. Shantaram was apparently financed by someone called Mr Gupta. We don't know too much about him. K.K. Puri, who is the father of India Today's proprietor, was one of the financiers for Raj Kapoor. They were not people whose names appeared on the credits of a film.'

Ranbir Raj Kapoor, the founder of R.K. Studio, was

born on 14 December 1924 in British India's Peshawar. His first stint in acting was as a child artiste in the 1935 film *Inquilab*. But in *Neel Kamal* (1947), Raj Kapoor got his biggest break as an actor in a role opposite Madhubala. The film turned Raj Kapoor into a star overnight, but that did not satisfy the young man. Just the way his father had established Prithvi Theatre, Raj Kapoor too wanted to start a similar organization but for films.

Raj Kapoor's son and actor and director Randhir Kapoor says, 'He was fond of acting and that's why he started his journey with Prithvi Theatre. But once he stepped into films, he developed a keen interest in film production and direction. And it was that interest that made him a studio owner, an equipment owner. It was all because of his passion for films.'

Thus in 1948, at a young age of just twenty-four, Raj Kapoor launched the banner of R.K. Films and made its first film *Aag* (1948). With that he became the youngest actor, producer and director of the country.

Although *Aag* launched the R.K. Studio banner but the film failed to garner success at the box office. Success came to Kapoor after his second film, *Barsaat* (1949). It is worth noting that *Barsaat* did a business of ₹1.1 crore at the box office back then, which in today's time is equivalent to ₹312 crore. With this financial success Raj Kapoor bought six acres of land in Chembur, where the structure of R.K. Studio was erected.

'With the grace of God, the film *Barsaat* did very well and whatever he earned from it, he invested in the studio,' says Randhir Kapoor. 'I remember my father used to always tell me that "people have used the earnings from films to make their bungalows; but I did not make bungalows and instead made this studio and bought its equipment because my hard work and passion was in filmmaking. Whatever I have earned from the films I have given that back to it."'

'Raj Kapoor always had a killer instinct. He had a high self-esteem. He was the first born of his father and had been playing with the camera from a young age. Yet, to think so big, to open a studio of his own, because his father never built his own studio, he had built Prithvi Theatre, was a matter of super confidence,' explains Bhawana Somaya, noted film journalist and author.

For Raj Kapoor, 1949 was an extremely successful year in every way. It was in that year that his work in *Andaz*, made under the direction of Mehboob Khan, got much appreciation. It too was a superhit film. Raj Kapoor could have easily continued to work as an actor if had desired so; but his focus was always more on filmmaking and his studio, than acting. In 1951, the third R.K. Studio film was released, which was incorporated in the *Time* magazine's list of All Time Top Ten Performances—*Awara*.

The importance of the film, from the commercial point of view, can be well understood from the fact that it broke the box office record set by *Barsaat* and did a business of about ₹1.25 crore. It was also during *Awara* that a particular signature of 'RK Films' was born.

Screenwriter Anjum Rajabali tells us that there was a desire that the Indian society should be one where there is a bit of socialism, equality, not too many caste differences, everybody's basic human rights and the dignity of their existence is maintained—this was definitely the vision of Nehru. The impact of that vision can be seen very transparently, especially in the films of R.K. Studio and those of that era.

While on the one hand the Hollywood of 50s was called the 'McCarthy Era' where people with Leftist and socialist ideology were getting blacklisted, on the other hand R.K. Films of Hindi cinema was moving forward in full vigour on the path of Nehruvian socialism. On paying attention, you would find that in every year of the 50s, the films of the Studio had this signature stamp and morality. Films like *Ab Dilli Door Nahi, Jagte Raho, Awara, Jis Desh Mein Ganga Behti Hai, Shree 420*, etc., are some such examples.

'If you watch every film from the 50s, they all have an underlined social issue, an aroma of Independent India,' adds Bhawana Somaya.

Randhir Kapoor says, 'the stories had a lot of passion and feelings in it, about a new Hindustan, a new India, which was coming up. This feeling was in everyone then. Not like today; we are not making those kinds of films today. That era was something else, the udaan [flight] was something else and the films were something else.'

Filmmaking is a collaborative art. R.K. Studio may have got its name from the name of its founder, but the morality and ideology of its films came from other companions—

writers K.A. Abbas and Rajinder Singh Bedi and lyricist Shailendra.

Talking about them, Anjum Rajabali says, 'Khwaja Ahmad Abbas was a complete progressive socialist. He was associated with IPTA (Indian People's Theatre Association). If you take a look at his films like *Naya Sansar* and *Dharti Ke Laal* and others which he had made, they were raw socialist documents. They were not great films, but his ideologies were everywhere in the content.'

Awara was made with the collaboration of K.A. Abbas and R.K. Studio, and it brought up a character which had no identity of its own. This became RK Studio's stamp—the tramp. 'Raj Kapoor had brought an image upon himself; the character of a tramp, which was a common man. He must have been inspired from Charlie Chaplin I am sure,' says Randhir Kapoor.

R.K. Studio presented the tramp in an Indian avatar. Elaborating on the character, Raj Kapoor had once said, 'The tramp had a greater identity with the common man. The element of hero worship is totally alien to the kind of sense of belonging I aspire to. Everybody can't be a Don Juan. While they see me in this image, they say "this man is like us".'

Actually, in most of R.K. Studio's films which came in the 50s this character appears in different forms again and again. In *Awara*, he was a misguided youth; in *Shree 420*, a human being stuck between 'vidya' (education) and 'maya' (wealth); in *Jis Desh Mein Ganga Behti Hai*, a man, who in spite of being surrounded by dacoits, was a picture of innocence.

'He is a lovable tramp. In a way, he is a misfit. He is a reject in the society but he still has ada and andaaz (style),' feels Anjum Rajabali, adding, 'There was certain panache, certain humour, even the charisma of the star which was allowed to appear (on screen). It was not cut out. So, the people used to feel that this man would come out of the situation in some way.'

The partnership between K.A. Abbas and R.K. Studio, which had started in 1951 with *Awara*, continued for the next forty years till Raj Kapoor's last film *Henna*.

While on the one hand R.K. Studio expressed its ideology through the character of the tramp, its songs on the other hand gave this expression more strength. Take for example the song *'Nanhe Munne Bachhe, Teri Mutthi Mei Kya Hai'* (What do you have in your fist, little child?) from the film *Boot Polish* (1954). Bhawana Somaya, who loves this song, says that Raj Kapoor had asked this question to Baby Naaz, the child actress in the song, who had replied: *'Mutthi mein hai takdeer humari* (we hold our destiny in our fist).'

'Cinema is a massive medium for multimedia expression and there are various elements that go into it such as performance, writing, lyrics and music. Raj Kapoor had a composite vision of all these, especially where each element reflected the other. So if his films were based on themes, like socialism and nation-building and other issues of the nation and its hopes, these songs would also reflect the same,' adds Anjum Rajabali.

Lyricist Shailendra is today referred to as the 'kaviraj' (great poet). His specialty was that he used to speak about big things in a small word. Look at the following example:

Mera joota hai japani,
ye patloon englistani,
sar pe laal topi roosi,
phir bhi dil hai Hindustani

(My shoes are from Japan,
This trouser is from England,
This red hat on my head is from Russia,
But my heart is still Indian)

(from *Shree 420*, 1955)

According to Rajabali, one may find the song simplistic but what it really meant was that all these different elements combined together form Hindustan, and this was an important comment in the films of that time. It was again the Nehruvian vision.

In the 50s, the way production house Navketan's initial films were given a soft, romantic and minimalistic music by S.D. Burman, the same way R.K. Studio's songs were given orchestra-centric melodies by Shankar-Jaikishan. Music historian Rajiv Vijayakar says, 'If we go back into time, [we'll see that] Ram Ganguly, who was the music composer for *Aag*, was signed for *Barsaat* (1949) also. But Raj Sahab's maternal uncle Vishwa Mehra told him that even in the film *Aag*, Shankar-Jaikishan had done a lot of work as assistants and their's was a major contribution. That was why Raj Kapoor signed them for *Barsaat*, and their association remained till *Mera Naam Joker* (1970) and *Kal Aaj aur Kal* (1971).

'Shankar-Jaikishan's first film as music composers was *Barsaat*, but their music style was set in *Awara*. Raj Kapoor even asked the poet Hasrat Jaipuri to leave his day job. He was a bus conductor and even after doing *Barsaat* he remained one because he was not confident of how he and his family would survive if he left his job. But Raj Sahab was confident about these four—Shailendra, Hasrat Jaipuri and Shankar-Jaikishan—that he got from them a stamp (style). At that time he probably did not even know that the pattern of the whole film industry would ultimately get influenced by it, and continue with the style of Shankar-Jaikishan in the 50s, 60s, 70s and further,' says Rajiv Vijayakar.

From *Aag* which came in 1948 to *Jagte Raho* in 1956, every film by the Studio had only one face—Nargis.

Anjum Rajabali says, 'You will find that Raj Kapoor's films had this mythical touch…that the character of a woman was either of a goddess or a temptress. He believed that a woman has these two sides. Therefore, you would also find sometimes that it's a composite character, that the same goddess is presented in a sensuous way, capturing her beauty and at the same time there was a strength of character. 'It is not a small thing that in many of his initial films Nargis played the lead role, and if you had seen Nargis in real life you'd have known that she did in fact have a certain strength of character, there was a solidity to her. R.K. Studio very easily used that feature and allowed it to spill over into the films. When you were casting Nargis in a film you had to write a character which was strong.' Rajabali adds.

R.K. Studio always gave immense importance to relationships. The Studio was known to have long partnerships with its technicians. Take Director of Photography (DoP) Radhu Karmarkar for example. He shot ten memorable films for the Studio and it also gave him his break as a director with *Jis Desh Mein Ganga Behti Hai* in 1960. Apart from Karmarkar, the studio gave a break to many other directors in the 50s. For instance, Prakash Arora, an assistant director for *Aag*, *Barsaat* and *Awara*, made *Boot Polish* in 1952, which got a Special Mention at the 1955 Cannes Film Festival. Similarly, Sombhu Mitra and Amit Maitra made *Jagte Raho* in 1956. The film was awarded the Crystal Globe (Grand Prix) at the Karlovy Vary International Film Festival in Czechoslovakia in 1957. It was a sheer coincidence that *Jagte Raho* was Nargis' last film with R.K. Studio.

'Not only as a director, but his vision as a filmmaker was pretty strong and definite. It was a part of him. Had Raj Kapoor been himself involved in *Boot Polish* or *Jagte Raho* or *Ab Dilli Door Nahi*, then he might have had the fear that his style and sensibility would overpower the film, not allowing it to move forward and then that quotient of modesty would not have been there,' says Anjum Rajabali.

Bhawana Somaya, however, feels that we look at it all with an eye for detail and over-analyse it, but actually it is all about simple business. If we have to run a studio there should be certain stories that are made within and some should come from outside and make good clean pictures.

By the 60s the foundation of Nehruvian socialism had become unsteady in the society. The definition of Hindi cinema too had changed. The films made were less in sync with the society. Escapist films were on the rise and cinema had become a source of mere entertainment, for example, *Hum Dono, Kohinoor, Love in Shimla, Nazrana, Manzil*, etc.

According to Ashish Rajadhyaksha, 'The Nehruvian ideal was seen to be worth pursuing. The 1962 War saw films, like *Haqeeqat,* and other of Chetan Anand's war movies. But it did see the end of that era. The filmmakers who supported the Left saw a series of further political splits, which lead to a new cinema emerging. I definitely see the end of Nehruvian period as the end of a kind of cinema which these filmmakers had also supported.'

With the change of time, the colour of the films of R.K. Studio also changed. In 1964 came one such film, which had absolutely no context with the prevalent social issues. It was an out-and-out entertainer, the first colour film by R.K. Studio—*Sangam*. In the mid 60s, Raj Kapoor did several films as an actor, such as *Around the World* in 1966 and *Sapno ka Saudagar* in 1968. However, these films didn't do well—neither critically, nor commercially. The Studio came under immense pressure. During the 60s, they had produced only a single film. In the 1970s, after the films he'd acted in having not done so well, Raj Kapoor once again turned towards his land of karma—R.K. Studio. He picked up the subject which was considered his magnum opus, his autobiographical film, the one that was closest to Kapoor's heart—*Mera Naam Joker*.

It took six long years in making. Studio owner Raj Kapoor put at stake everything that he had for the film. Even the Studio itself was mortgaged for it. When released in the theatres, *Mera Naam Joker* was 255-minute-long. The film had two intervals. The critics liked the film and Raj Kapoor even received the Filmfare Award for the Best Director. But look at the strange game played by destiny: his masterpiece became his biggest flop at the box office.

Randhir Kapoor elaborates on this, 'The concept of *Mera Naam Joker* is very Western—that the show must go on; the saga of smiling through tears. Maybe in those days, people did not understand it.'

Bhawana Somaya adds, '*Mera Naam Joker* did not do well at all. Raj Kapoor was so shocked that he was in a massive depression. He was highly disappointed that people did not understand his film and the artiste within him.'

'The financial loss was huge,' admits Randhir Kapoor, adding that there even came a day when they thought they might have to sell the Studio. 'But the circumstances were okay and my mother came out and helped, and we sold off everything that we had—the property, jewellery, and everything that was there, we sold off. Every creditor was paid to the last single paisa. My mother said that we would sell everything but the Studio. She said whatever we had earned was off the Studio. So the Studio should be saved,' says Randhir Kapoor.

Raj Kapoor was also severely disappointed. Though he continued directing and producing films for the Studio, but as an actor *Mera Naam Joker* was his last film with it.

When the 70s began, the stars of R.K. Studio weren't favourable. The Studio desperately needed a hit film to overcome the mental and financial losses due to *Mera Naam Joker*. On the other hand, times had changed and the stars had changed. It was the era of Rajesh Khanna. Raj Kapoor was soon going to be fifty years old and the Studio needed a hit star.

Randhir Kapoor further says that many bigwigs of the industry came forward to help Raj Kapoor during the hard times. Then one day Raj Kapoor told him that he was starting a new tasveer (film). He asked his mother if she could give him her young boy. She asked what it was about. He then told her about wanting to make *Bobby* with Rishi.

In this do-or-die moment in the history of R.K. Studio, Raj Kapoor surprised everyone by choosing to make a film about a teenage love story with two debutants. Like they say, luck favours the brave. *Bobby*, which came in 1973, was the biggest hit film of that year, and still has its name in the list of top box office hits of Hindi cinema.

'It was always a one-man show, he just wanted to prove a point,' says Randhir Kapoor. He adds with a smile, 'He made *Bobby* and it was such a big sixer that the ball went straight out of the stadium. It was our biggest box office hit.'

'Raj Kapoor had the last laugh,' says Bhawana Somaya,

'because this was not a film of his temperament. But he wanted to prove that no matter how old he had become, his heart still beats like Bobby's, that he understands teenage love story because love never changes.'

On a cursory glance one may not notice it but if one looks deep into it they'll see that here too the film's screenwriter and R.K. Studio's old insider K.A. Abbas's socialist ideologies can be seen as the foundation of the story.

'If you take a look at Bobby's father, Premnath's character, you will find certain shades of *Awara*'s title character. He is a poor man but a man of dignity, a man of hope, a man of struggle. He is a man who can hold his own in front of the rich people,' explains Rajabali.

The scene in *Bobby* where Rishi Kapoor meets Dimple Kapadia for the first time was inspired from Raj Kapoor's real life. It is said that that's how he had first met Nargis. *Bobby* changed the definition of romance in Hindi cinema. It introduced the genre of runaway teenage love stories. On the one hand, the success of *Bobby* gave a new lease of life to R.K. Studio, but on the other the film also became its last great achievement.

'R.K. Studio by then had become mostly a place for hire. Kapoor himself used to make a film once every three or five years or whenever he got drawn to it. It was not something that he needed to do, so he would make his films whenever he chose to. By this time he had become something of a legend and was living life pretty much the way he wanted to,' says Ashish Rajadhyaksha.

After the success of *Bobby*, only two films were made in

the 70s at R.K. Studio—*Dharam Karam* and *Satyam Shivam Sundaram*. No outsider director made a film at R.K. Studio. The Studio had become a one-man show.

'The difference between Hollywood and Bollywood was that most of our studios, especially the more impactful ones, were all led by filmmakers,' observes Anjum Rajabali. If we look at Hollywood studios like Warner Brothers, Columbia Pictures, etc., the architects of those were not filmmakers.

Here the filmmakers had made their own studios. Dev Anand, Guru Dutt, Bimal Roy, Raj Kapoor—all of them. Since these studios were led by filmmakers that is why their individual vision or stamp reflected on the studios, whereas in Hollywood the stamp of studios came upon the films.

R.K. Studio's films which came during and after mid-70s kept trying to give a message to the society: the conflict between physical and spiritual love, widow remarriage, the issues of Indo-Pak friendship. But then commercial requirements had taken over the issues of these films, for example, *Satyam Shivam Sundaram* (1978), *Ram Teri Ganga Maili* (1985), *Henna* (1991), etc.

'If you focus on the entertainment quotient, personal stories and love stories began taking prominence over other themes and within it the woman's character started acquiring much more sensuality as it moved on,' says Anjum Rajabali. 'Thereon, his films began to be known more for its display of the sensuality of the female characters and less for its content. This became the hallmark. The Studio's focus mindset began changing and the people's mindset towards it also began changing,' he adds.

During the shooting of *Henna* in 1987, Raj Kapoor was bestowed upon with the India's highest award in cinema—the Dadasaheb Phalke Award. He passed away in 1988.

With the passing away of Raj Kapoor, somewhere the will of the people associated with the Studio also broke. For the next three years no film came from the Studio. In the 90s, although his three sons made a film each—*Henna* (Randhir Kapoor), *Prem Granth* (Rajiv Kapoor), *Aa Ab Laut Chalen* (Rishi Kapoor), but the glory of R.K. Studio could not be restored to what it was before.

According to Bhawana Somaya, 'Those films did not do well. They were not as good as Raj Kapoor's, but so what? You have to keep doing films. But in this case, the sons cannot be blamed because all of them, especially Rishi Kapoor, were very busy with their acting projects so it was very difficult to direct films as a full-time job.'

Anjum Rajabali says, 'Not only vision, but the energy, the sensibility, the whole architecture of the vision—where was it coming from? It was coming from a single individual. He was the one who determined that and those times were such. It was not a corporate era where there are board meetings, or a committee sitting down and deciding which script is good and which is not. Only one man was there. And Raj Kapoor was so larger than life that after him it became virtually impossible for his sons Randhir and Rishi Kapoor (although Rishi Kapoor was probably not as much involved with the Studio) to take things forward and they could not do it.'

Talking about it, Randhir Kapoor says that they too feel that the gap was too long, which should not have been the case and he takes the blame for it instead of passing it onto others. 'We did not make them [films] and that's our mistake,' he admits.

R.K. Studio's filming style and its hold on ideology inspired many big filmmakers in Hindi cinema and this stamp is clearly visible on their films, for example, *3 Idiots* and *Munna Bhai MBBS*. 'Many people tried to emulate the style and to an extent were successful at it too,' says Anjum Rajabali. 'If you take a look at Subhash Ghai's films, especially of his golden period, he too had a similar grandeur. Maybe the same ideology wasn't there; the same morality or flavour of political content may not be there; but he maintained the grandeur, the song and dance and the huge mounting. The same showmanship. But in R.K. Studio, along with the showmanship there used to be relevant content too,' he adds.

If we compare R.K Studio with its contemporaries, like Navketan Studios, Rajkamal Kala Mandir and Bombay Talkies, it becomes obvious that R.K. Studio is the only studio left which still has stars, studio space and infrastructure. R.K. Studio is the only studio which has a ray of hope of restarting.

Randhir Kapoor says they plan to restart some work soon. And once again there will be a romance which will be recreated between the audience and them.

A famous song from Raj Kapoor's *Mera Naam Joker* sums up the illustrious R.K. Studio's journey:

Jeena Yahan, Marna Yahan,
Iske Siwa, Jana Kahan?

(You live here, you die here
But for here, where else can one go?)

FILMOGRAPHY

Aag (1948)
Barsaat (1949)
Awara (1951)
Aah (1953)
Boot Polish (1954)
Shree 420 (1955)
Jagte Raho (1956)
Ab Dilli Dur Nahi (1957)
Jis Desh Mein Ganga Behti Hai (1960)
Sangam (1964)
Mera Naam Jokar (1970)
Kal Aaj aur Kal (1971)
Bobby (1973)
Dharam Karam (1975)
Satyam Shivam Sundaram (1978)
Biwi O Biwi (1981)
Prem Rog (1982)
Ram Teri Ganga Maili (1985)
Henna (1991)
Prem Granth (1996)
Aa Ab Laut Chalen (1999)

9
NAVKETAN FILMS
Introducing the Urban Hero

Founders: Chetan Anand and Dev Anand

The longest term in the studio era—61 years, 36 films.

The three brothers were the pillars of the studio—Dev, Chetan and Vijay Anand.

The studio for the first time introduced an urban hero in Indian films.

A hint of Hollywood inspiration could be seen in the films.

Memorable, soft, lilting and romantic music, and later path-breaking Western music.

Symbolized the newly independent India and the rising middle-class.

Every studio makes a number of films in its lifetime, but usually it's that one film which gets etched in the minds of the audience and in the pages of history. Navketan Films released their masterpiece in 1965, the film which *Time* magazine placed at the number four position in the Bollywood Classics of All Time—*Guide*.

For majority of the audience, *Guide* alone remains the identity of Navketan Films. But legendary studios are not made with one or two masterpieces, it takes a body of work over a long period of time to achieve the cult status. With thirty-six films in the period between 1950–2011, Navketan Films has had the longest run amongst all its contemporaries. The studio with its progressive thoughts on modern India became the representative of the middle-class.

Journalist and author Siddharth Bhatia says, 'The films which were made between 1950 and 1965, were mostly themed on nation-building and had a subtle message about India, its villages, social reforms and socialism. If you take a look at Raj Kapoor's films, the stories of which were written by K.A. Abbas, they had ordinary themes about the rich harassing the poor, etc. Unlike the films made by V. Shantaram (*Do Ankhen Barah Haath*), Bimal Roy (*Do Beegha Zameen*), Mehboob Khan (*Mother India*), Navketan's films were urban in their elements, which were made in the cities. Its stories were about migrants where the hero belonged to the lower middle-class, a working class and he lived in a city.' Bhatia adds that this theme was very specific to Navketan Films.

The beginning of Navketan's journey of dreams was from the collaboration of two brothers, in the year 1950. The younger of the two, Dev Anand, had worked in Bombay Talkies' *Ziddi* in 1948 and had instantly earned the tag of a rising star. Elder brother Chetan Anand was associated with the Leftist background of IPTA. In 1946, as a director for his first independent film, *Neecha Nagar*, he won the Grand Prix du Festival International du Film award at the Cannes Film Festival—it was the first Indian film to have won an award at the festival. And when the talented actor and director duo came together, it marked the start of Navketan Films

Journalist and author Bhawana Somaaya explains, 'The brothers felt that in order to make films of their taste, where they could show what they wanted to and where no one else could order them to edit this and keep that, they must start their own banner. They decided to name the company after Chetan Anand's son, Ketan. "Nav" means new, and the idea was to start a new kind of cinema. So, the name "Navketan" was chosen.'

Most studios of the time owned the land they were built on. Rajkamal Kalamandir was established in Lower Parel, Mumbai. R.K. Studios had its own six acres of land in Chembur. Contrary to this trend, Navketan Films used to operate from director Mehboob Khan's Mehboob Studio.

Film producer Amit Khanna tells us that the brothers had bought a huge plot of land in Goregaon in the early 50s but due to some legal complications, they could not get its possession. Although Dev Anand had not worked with Mehboob Khan until then but the latter was quite fond of Dev Anand and allowed the brothers to operate Navketan Films out of Mehboob Studio. Dev Anand was the only actor to whom Mehboob Khan had given his own make-up room. However, Navketan had its own green room and a godown, among other facilities.

In 1950 came the first film by the studio—*Afsar*, which was an adaptation of Russian author Nikolai Gogol's satirical play, *The Inspector General*. This film had the same tone as Chetan Anand's *Neecha Nagar* and was seen propagating his Leftist ideology.

Siddharth Bhatia tells us that the film cannot be found today because its prints had burnt. He, however, has seen its two portions and calls it a very 'stagey film'. Chetan Anand's initial two to three films appeared as if they were shot on a stage theatre.

Afsar failed at the box office, which was a rude shock to the studio. On the other hand, Dev Anand, a rising star of that time, needed a blockbuster. In 1951, came the second film by Navketan—*Baazi*, which proved to be a game-changer for the studio.

Amit Khanna shares an anecdote, 'Amidst all his contemporaries, Dev Anand was the most forward-thinking actor along with Guru Dutt. Very few people know that both were huge fans of Hollywood films and they regularly watched them. So, *Baazi* was the first film in which you could see the direct influence of Hollywood.

Many new things were introduced in the film, like the

character of a vamp. Another new feature was a cabaret kind of music, which too was a first for the audience.

Baazi was the debut film of director Guru Dutt. After the failure of the first film of the studio, to let a new filmmaker make the second one was quite a bold decision but there is a story behind it too. According to Siddharth Bhatia, 'Both, Dev Anand and Guru Dutt, met at Prabhat Studios. Guru Dutt was the dance master there and Dev Anand was trying for more roles, while working in a film. The washerman got their shirts mixed-up, and eventually they realized that they were wearing each other's shirts. From then on, they became friends and promised to take each other in their first directorial/production venture. This is how Guru Dutt happened to direct *Baazi*.'

With the success of *Baazi* the foundation of the studio became stronger. Thus, Chetan Anand tried to return to his ideological landing. In 1952 came *Aandhiyan* and in 1953 came *Humsafar*. Sadly, these two films met the same fate as *Afsar*.

Amit Khanna tells us, '*Aandhiyan* was a very realistic film, which was appreciated a lot. Prabhu Dayal, an old associate of Dev Anand and Guru Dutt from their days in Prabhat Studios, was invited to its premiere. He was a blunt man, and after the show when Dev Anand asked him, "Prabhuji, how did you like the film?"

'Dayal questioned back, "What is the duration of the film?"

'Dev Anand replied, "Two and a half hours."

'Prabhu Dayal promptly said, "This film will run for two and quarter hours."

'It was a very artistic film. It was sent to Venice and appreciated there by all. There was Ali Akbar Khan's music in it. But the film bombed when it came to box office.'

With the failure of *Aandhiyan* and *Humsafar*, once again doubts cropped up regarding the sustenance of the newborn studio. They desperately needed a hit film, which ultimately resulted in Chetan Anand having to change his way of filmmaking. *Taxi Driver*, which came in 1954, was truly a family affair. It is possible that in the history of cinema, this was the only instance where the director was the eldest brother, Chetan Anand, lead actor was the middle brother, Dev Anand, and the writer was the youngest brother, Vijay Anand.

Amit Khanna adds, 'Both the brothers realized that if they do not make commercially successful films then they would not be able to sustain their studio. Within fifteen days, Vijay Anand wrote a storyline. He was studying at St. Xavier's College then and was interested in theatre. In it too you can see the influence of *Baazi* and that of Hollywood thrillers. *Taxi Driver* was shot within twenty-seven days. It had beautiful songs created by S.D. Burman and Sahir Ludhianvi. If you consider the aesthetics and the rest in *Taxi Driver*, it looks a lot like today's thriller films, even after sixty years. It was a huge hit.'

This marked the beginning of the successful era of Navketan Films. But destiny had some other plans in store.

Gradually, a wall developed between Dev Anand and Chetan Anand's professional relationship. It is believed that by then Dev Anand had achieved stardom and was mostly interested in commercial films, whereas Chetan Anand was still fixated with his Leftist ideologies. After *Funtoosh* came out in 1956, Chetan Anand parted ways with the studio and started his own banner—Himalaya Films.

A turning point came in Navketan when the youngest brother, Vijay Anand, took over the reins from Chetan Anand and handled the studio through its golden years.

In 1957, at the young age of just twenty-four, Vijay Anand, fondly known as Goldie, made his first film for Navketan, a fine piece of work by the young, forward-thinking director—*Nau Do Gyarah*. Then in 1963, under his direction, came *Tere Ghar Ke Samne*, which is widely considered the first romantic comedy film of Hindi cinema.

According to Siddharth Bhatia, 'Of the three brothers, Vijay Anand was the most influenced by Hollywood. His films were clearly inspired: in their sleekness, techniques and stories. If you watch the film *Teesri Manzil*, the influence is obvious in it. And *Tere Ghar Ke Samne*, which has vanished from people's memory, is a romantic comedy inspired from Hollywood too—it shows parental pressure but there are no sad sequences, so that fun feel of a "romcom" can be seen there.'

Nau Do Gyarah, *Kala Bazar* and *Tere Ghar Ke Samne* proved that Vijay Anand and Navketan Films were tied to a particular genre. By the age of twenty-nine, Vijay Anand was amongst the top directors of Hindi cinema.

Amit Khanna explains, 'Vijay Anand created a distinct style of song picturization. He is very underestimated. People give more credit to Guru Dutt. But Guru Dutt had used that same lineage and taken it further. I don't think there is any director in India who can do a better song picturization till date. He used to, intuitively, keep the camera at the correct place. Camera movement which we call "mise-en-scene" was actually first introduced in India by Navketan.'

The credit of building the urban image of Navketan goes to the modern and forward thinking of Dev and Vijay Anand. On the same lines, the credit to bring about the personality of the urban hero goes to the contemporary modern music of those films which was S.D. Burman's creation.

Siddharth Bhatia tells us, 'S.D. Burman was leaving Mumbai in the 50s because he hadn't been very successful and nobody cared for his brand of music. But he was requested to stay back and compose for *Baazi*. After *Baazi* became a success, S.D. Burman dropped his plans of leaving Mumbai. Then onwards, he was always the one to create music for all of Navketan's films, with the exception of *Hum Dono*, until *Haré Rama Haré Krishna*. The brothers had complete faith in him, they would make some suggestions here and there but they never asked S.D. Burman to make music in a certain way. They would just leave things upto him.'

Musician Ranjit Barot says, 'S.D. Burman's inspiration was Bengali folk music from where the feel in all his songs came. Even the instrumentation is very soft and romantic—clouds, ankle bells—it was not abrasive. It was not an aggressive sound. Actually his most aggressive music came later when his son R.D. Burman used to arrange music for him.'

If you see *Jewel Thief*, there is a complete modern take from there, which happened because of R.D. Burman. *Afsar*, which came in 1950, to *Tere Mere Sapne* in 1971, S.D. Burman did twelve films for the studio where the range of his songs could be seen.

Music historian Rajiv Vijayakar says, 'Look at Dilip [Kumar] Sahab and Naushad, look at this combination; and look at Raj [Kapoor] Sahab and Shankar-Jaikishan's combination. So, it was amazing but used to revolve around in a limit. But there was no such limit for S.D. Burman and Dev Anand. He used to work with only the fixed 4–5 singers for Dev Anand. Although outside of Navketan Films, S.D. Burman worked with Mukesh and Manna Dey and Bhupinder Singh. But for the studio's films, his regulars remained Mohammad Rafi, Talat Mahmood and Hemant Kumar—there was a huge variety in it and such freshness. When this combination came together that is when we knew that it was modern young music.'

Although the triangle of Dev Anand, Vijay Anand and S.D. Burman made many wonderful films but their biggest hit was yet to come on the silver screen, in 1965 to be specific. During that time the atmosphere in the country was pretty conservative. The Indian woman felt trapped in the boundaries of shame, shyness and meekness. In such an environment came Navketan's *Guide*, which brought the morality of the society in the witness box. Based on R.K. Narayan's novel, *Guide* is the story of Rosy who is disheartened by her husband and her marriage, and finds solace in the arms of a simpleton Raju Guide.

Amit Khanna says, 'The story of the film *Guide* actually starts from the 1962 Berlin Film Festival. *Hum Dono* was India's official entry to it. Nobel Laureate Pearl S. Buck was on the jury. She had liked the film a lot. She got to meet Dev Anand and Vijay Anand and suggested that they should make a film in India which she would script. She said there is a story by the author R.K. Narayan—*The Guide*, which she liked.'

Dev Anand contacted R.K. Narayan in Mysore and the rights were bought. There were two version of the film to be made. The English version was to be made by American-Polish film director Tad Danielewski, whom Pearl S. Buck had roped in. They were writing the script for the American audience and they had prepared a 'touristy' script for that. When Vijay Anand came on board, he felt that this film would not do because it was peripheral. There was no story, no emotions, no scope for songs—he then re-wrote the script.

Bhawana Somaaya adds, '*Guide* was supposed to be directed by Chetan Anand. But since a long time he had been trying to get permission to shoot his film *Haqeeqat*. On the other hand, preparations for *Guide* were on. When he got the permission, Chetan Anand put his hands up and said, "I am going to shoot my film." So, Dev Anand turned to Vijay Anand and said, "Okay Goldie, you are the man. You are going to direct *Guide*."

Although the film's name was *Guide*, the star of the film was Dev Anand, but for me it was the story of Rosy, of every Indian woman who wanted to live life at her own terms; who wanted to break free.

According to Bhawana Somaaya, 'The character of Rosy describes how an Indian woman should have been defined in that era. The scene where she takes the fire-torch and goes to the cave where her husband is spending time with another girl and says, "Marco, *main jeena chahti hun* (Marco, I want to live)"—that is not just Rosy's voice, it is the voice of every Indian woman who wants to live for herself and not treat her husband as God.'

Amongst Hindi films, *Guide* was the first to win Filmfare Awards in all the major four categories—Best Actor, Best Actress, Best Director and Best Film. For its first ten weeks, all the shows of *Guide* went houseful in Mumbai's Maratha Mandir theatre. The film celebrated a silver jubilee in Ahmedabad and even when Gujarat was struggling with a famine, people would pray before the posters of '*Guide* prays for rain.'

It is common practice today, but back then *Guide* was the first film for which processes like casting direction, special effects, screen tests, etc., were all carried out. Bhanu Athaiya, who later went to win an Oscar for another film, did the costume designing for *Guide*. Since, the unit had been brought from Hollywood...the cameramen had to be selected. The top 6–7 cameramen of the industry gave tests for the selection—Radhu Karmakar, Subroto Mitra, Fardoon Irani, Nariman Irani, Jal Mistry and Fali Mistry. Ultimately, Fali Mistry was chosen and his work in the film became a benchmark. The film was processed in New York's Pathé Labs, the prints were made there in America. *Guide* was an expensive film, back then it was sold at ₹10 lakh per territory, which was the second highest price after *Mughal-E-Azam*.

When the film released, its initial report wasn't very good. It was disheartening for Navketan Films, but soon the circumstances turned favourable and things picked up the second week onwards. It went on to mark its silver and golden jubilees at several theatres and won many accolades.

By this time differences began cropping up between Dev and Vijay Anand. It is said that this was the beginning of the decline of Navketan Films in the years to come.

Siddharth Bhatia tells us that both the brothers wanted to do different things, 'Goldie used to say he wants to act but he was not an actor. Dev Anand wanted to direct but he was not a great director. This led to differences between them and they parted ways. They did make one or two odd films later, like *Chhupa Rustam*, etc., but the magic was gone.'

In 1971, came the last film of the combination of Dev Anand and Vijay Anand for Navketan—*Tere Mere Sapne*, based on A.J. Cronin's novel, *The Citadel*. But *Tere Mere Sapne* failed to conjure magic at the box office and with it Vijay Anand bid farewell to the studio. Incidentally,

Tere Mere Sapne was also the last Navketan film with S.D. Burman. After the departure of Vijay Anand and S.D. Burman, Navketan's spirits were gradually dying. The studio needed a new lease of life.

It was a break or make moment for Navketan Films. And at this critical juncture, in 1971 came *Haré Rama Haré Krishna*. It not only gave Navketan a new breath of life but also reinvented and revolutionalized the music in Hindi cinema.

Amit Khanna shares an interesting incident behind the making of *Haré Rama Haré Krishna*. 'One day, I got a call from Dev Anand saying that I am going to Nepal to attend the wedding of the crown prince. So after ten fifteen days he got a telegram, it said can you receive me at the hotel on so and so day and book a hotel for me because I finalized a script. So, I arranged for a hotel and went to receive him and there he said that he has written a story about hippies—*Haré Rama Haré Krishna*.'

R.D. Burman, fondly known as Pancham, was the music director of *Haré Rama Haré Krishna*. Pancham was a child prodigy who had composed his first song at the age of nine. Incidentally, S.D. Burman had used it in Navketan's 1955 film *Funtoosh*.

According to Rajiv Vijayakar, 'Dev Anand had gone to Dada Burman and asked him to compose all the serious songs in the film, but the two Western songs needed can be composed by Pancham. S.D. Burman did not agree to this, he replied: "Why? My son can do all the songs." And that is what happened, because even without "*Dum Maro Dum*", *Haré Rama Haré Krishna* is a landmark square. It is probably the square which is amongst the top five in Pancham's career.'

Through *Haré Rama Haré Krishna*, for the first time hippie culture was shown in Hindi films. It showed young people experimenting with gurus, music, sex and drugs and the protagonist, Janice a.k.a. Jasmeet, surrounded by it all. At that time, neither did a mainstream actress wanted to play the controversial role of Janice nor that of Dev Anand's sister. Therefore, Navketan Films took the risk of casting a new face—Zeenat Aman.

Amit Khanna says that the casting of Zeenat Aman was coincidental. Dev Anand had done a film for 20th Century Fox back then, which very few people know about. The title of the film was *Evil Within*. It had the role of an Indian girl, which Zeenat Aman had played. She had just won the title of Miss Asia Pacific. Dev Anand liked her in that film and decided to cast her.

Bhawana Somaaya reveals that Dev Anand was an expert in discovering new actors and according to her, Zeenat Aman was his most sensational discovery, 'Though she signed the film, Zeenat Aman was not very confident about becoming a heroine and was packing her bags. Dev Anand requested her to wait for just two months till *Haré Rama Haré Krishna* released, and if she still feels the same after it she could leave. She was ready to leave for Germany with her mother. But the film released and became a blockbuster hit.'

Haré Rama Haré Krishna garnered enormous success and in 1971, Zeenat Aman got the Filmfare Award for Best Supporting Actress.

Although from 1978 to 2011 Dev Anand kept making films for Navketan, but either he did not realize that he was growing old or he did not understand the changing taste of the audience—whatever may have been the reason, after 1978 the decline of Navketan had begun.

Amit Khanna says, 'Dev Anand couldn't understand the kind of films which were being made in that period. So, he would make his own but in a disconnected way. When times change, you have to change with it. You cannot remain static, there is always a transition. But Navketan Films became stagnant.'

Bhawana Somaaya adds, 'Dev Anand was getting old, but he kept playing the central character because of which his films never had any impact.'

In 2002, Dev Anand was awarded the Dadasaheb Phalke Award and after nine more years of making films he passed away in 2011.

Thirty-six films in sixty-one years. In the studio era, Navketan had the longest life. Its contribution to Hindi cinema is no less than any other studio.

According to Siddharth Bhatia, 'Navketan Films was modern, it was urban in terms of style. It was progressive in its own way. Even today the same kind: crime and urban-centric films are being made. If Dev Anand had not been there, then Shammi Kapoor could not have been there either and if Shammi Kapoor would not have been there then Rajesh Khanna, Aamir Khan or Shahrukh Khan would not have been there too. It's a sequence of style continuing from those days.'

'The biggest contribution of Navketan is Dev Anand himself,' says Bhawana Somaaya, 'After that would be Vijay Anand and S.D. Burman. Burman cannot be forgotten because he and Dev Anand were the two sides of the same coin. You can't figure out where S.D. Burman ends and where Dev Anand starts.'

Amit Bhatia adds, 'Its melodious music and poetry is such that it enraptures the hearts of people even today. Also, the number of immensely talented people whom Navketan introduced to the film industry no other banner had done.'

The various aspects of Navketan are still as attractive. The studio gave Hindi cinema a new urban hero, unforgettable music, a new definition of entertainment, new genre and most importantly a break to forty-five new people in the industry, which also included director Raj Khosla who began his career by assisting Guru Dutt in *Baazi* and I assisted Raj Khosla. Thus, it can be said that the glow of the light ignited by Navketan is still reaching people through mere mortals like me and would continue to do so.

FILMOGRAPHY

Afsar (1950)
Baazi (1951)
Aandhiyan (1952)
Humsafar (1953)
Taxi Driver (1955)
House No. 44 (1955)
Funtoosh (1956)
Kala Pani (1958)
Kala Bazar (1960)
Hum Dono (1961)
Tere Ghar Ke Samne (1963)
Guide (1965)
Jewel Thief (1967)
Prem Pujari (1970)
Tere Mere Sapne (1971)
Haré Raama Haré Krishna (1971)
Shareef Budmaash (1973)
Heera Panna (1973)
Ishq Ishq Ishq (1974)
Jaaneman (1976)
Des Pardes (1978)
Lootmaar (1980)
Swami Dada (1982)
Anand Aur Anand (1984)
Awwal Number (1990)
Pyaar Ka Tarana (1993)
Gangster (1994)

Main Solah Baras Ki (1998)
Censor (2001)
Love at Times Square (2003)
Mr Prime Minister (2005)
Chargesheet (2011)

10
BIMAL ROY PRODUCTIONS
Where Art Meets Business

Founder: Bimal Roy (1909–65)

15 films in 14 years.

Seven Filmfare Awards for Best Director.

Four Filmfare Awards for Best Film.

Winner of one National Award for Best Film.

International prize winner at Cannes Film Festival.

Its films identified with themes of social justice, great performances and melodious music.

Amazing amalgamation of art and business.

The 1950s was a transitional phase in Hindi cinema. The streams of regional talent from Lahore, Bengal and other corners of the country were joining the mainstream Hindi cinema after Partition. Mumbai had become the centre of Indian cinema.

At this point, came a name from the land of Bengal who became the representative of Bengali culture and aesthetics in Hindi cinema—Bimal Roy, who also went on to represent Indian cinema on international platforms through his studio, Bimal Roy Productions.

Bimal Roy was born on 12 July 1909 to a zamindar family in Suapur, Dhaka, which was part of the then East India province of British India. After the death of his father, at the age of nineteen he moved to Kolkata from his village.

Rinki Bhattacharya, daughter and official biographer of Bimal Roy, tells us that Bimal Roy had six brothers and he was the eldest of them all. 'He was all of nineteen and studying at Jagannath College in Dhaka, which is a very reputed college even today, when my grandfather passed away. When the Nayab there told him that his father had left a huge amount of debt behind and that he should either pay up the money or leave, he had nobody to consult with. He had to himself take the decision overnight. He chose to leave for Kolkata with his mother and two brothers, and did everything that came his way just to keep the family going.'

Bimal Roy's Hindi films are famous all over the world even today. But very few people know that the journey of his dreams started in Bengal.

New Theatres was the hub of Bengali cinema at that

time. It was there that Bimal Roy got his first job in the film business. He was hired as a publicity photographer, and gradually worked his way to becoming a cinematographer there.

According to Rinki Bhattacharya, 'He had opened up a small still studio on Lansdowne Road (now Sarat Bose Road), Kolkata, where all the eminent people would go to be photographed. All the heroines would line up to get photographed by Bimal Roy; it was then that he was noticed by Nitin Bose who became just like a mentor to him.'

Bimal Roy's first job in the studio was as the director of photography (DOP) for the 1937 film, *Mukti*. His work at New Theatres was much appreciated. In 1944, he got his directorial break—for which he chose a risky theme. At that time New Theatres was making films on only social, literary and mythological themes. Distancing himself from all these Bimal Roy made the first political film of Bengal—*Udayer Pathey* (Towards the Light).

Film writer Anjum Rajabali says, 'Bengal is often associated with intellect and politics, and Bengalis are generally well-read people, inclined towards literature and art. They debate a lot and have clear and emphatic views on politics. Since Bimal Roy himself came from that intellectual culture, it is not so surprising that he put forth his statement with belief and courage.'

Udayer Pathey was a grand success both critically and commercially. The film went houseful for a very long time at Kolkata's Chitra cinema hall. The craze for the film was so much that without the help of police it used to be very difficult to control the crowd. Looking at its popular appeal, New Theatres made a Hindi version of the film that very year: *Hamrahi*, which also went on to become so popular that for the first time in Indian films its dialogues were transferred to audio discs and marketed.

In 1947, India became independent, Bengal got divided and the Bengali audience also got divided into two. Thus, the pioneer of Bengali cinema, New Theatres, saw a decline in its business. In 1950, inspired by Subhas Chandra Bose's life, *Pehla Aadmi*, was the last film by Bimal Roy for New Theatres.

And the very same year, Bimal Roy took his entire team comprising Hrishikesh Mukherjee, Nabendu Ghosh, Asit Sen, Kamal Bose and Salil Chowdhury and moved to Mumbai.

In 1952, Bimal Roy directed the film *Maa*, produced by Bombay Talkies, which was based on the Hollywood film *Over The Hills*. In 1953, he returned to his native Bengal and made a film based on the novel of his favourite novelist, Sarat Chandra Chatterjee, for which he got the Filmfare for Best Director—*Parineeta*, following which Bimal Roy got a foothold in the Bombay film industry.

'He loved love stories,' says Rinki Bhattacharya, adding, 'What brought him to this story was the unspoken relationship between the man and the woman. So, the name Parineeta itself is indicative of the fact that she is given away to somebody else and she doesn't belong to anyone now.

He had definitely looked at it from a feminist point of view.'

Bimal Roy had become a successful director. But big achievements come with small steps. It was a spontaneous decision that led him to take the biggest step of his life—establishing his own film studio.

According to Rinki Bhattacharya, 'It happened after the first International Festival Film Festival of India, where he watched Vittorio De Sica's *Bicycle Thieves* and *Miracle in Milan*. Later one day, while he was returning home with his team, lost in his thoughts, he suddenly asked, "Why can't we make films like those?" Everybody, including his assistants, were there and they said, "Yes, we can." To which he asked, "Who will write it?" And Hrishi Da [Hrishikesh Mukherjee] said, "I will write it." And just like that they started the production house.'

The owner of Mohan Studios, Ramneek Bhai, respected Bimal Roy a lot and offered him his own studio for shooting. So, it was from Mohan Studios that Bimal Roy Productions operated. In fact it came to be known as Bimal Roy's studio. Nobody knew it didn't belong to him. Similarly, today we know Salil Chowdhury as a great music composer. But what is interesting is that, in 1953, it was he who had penned the first draft of the script of the Bimal Roy Productions'—*Do Bigha Zamin*, which was inspired from Tagore's poem 'Dui Beegha Jomi'.

Do Bigha Zamin was the story of a farmer in a village, Shambhu, who was laden with debt, in order to repay which he moves to Kolkata to look for work and in the struggle to get his land back loses everything he had. Bimal Roy had seen poor farmers getting harassed by rich landowners during his childhood. He had seen the caste differentiation. The impact of these social inequalities on him could be seen in *Do Bigha Zamin*.

Anjum Rajabali says, 'Although Bimal Roy was born and brought up in a landowner's family and was an elite in the power structure there, his personal sensitivity and ideology was absolutely against that system. We can believe that this man became an artiste and a filmmaker as a reaction must have awakened in him to the prevalent exploitation, giving him grief and if he was to protest against it, he had to find an expression and that's probably what brought him into filmmaking.'

'Interestingly, Balraj Sahni had not ever played a character even to close to the one he did in *Do Bigha Zamin*. One always imagined him in a coat and tie, suit and boot, but never in a dhoti or torn shirt and pulling a rickshaw. He had never portrayed a villager. But what a wonderful job he has done there and what a right choice he was for that role; he had delivered a truly inspiring performance,' adds Rajabali.

Commercially speaking, *Do Bigha Zamin* wasn't very successful but it was a massive success in the award circle. Beating films like *Anarkali*, *Footpath*, *Aurat* and Mehboob Khan's *Aan* which also came in the same year, *Do Bigha Zamin* bagged the Filmfare Award for Best Film and Best Director. For its powerful social message, the film was also honoured with the Prize for Social Progress at the Karlovy Vary International Film Festival. It also became the first Indian film to win the International Prize at the Cannes Film Festival, in 1954.

After the national and international success of the first film of the studio, the star of Bimal Roy Productions was shining at its brightest. However, the next three films which came in 1954: *Naukri*, *Baap Beti* and *Biraj Bahu*, also critically acclaimed, were not commercially successful. The studio desperately needed a hit film. At this critical juncture, Bimal Roy once again turned towards Bengali literature and made a remake of the film on which he had once worked as the cameraman—*Devdas*.

It is from there that the collaboration between Bimal Roy Productions and Dilip Kumar began. Films like *Shaheed*, *Andaz*, *Deedar* and *Aan* had made Dilip Kumar the biggest star of the time. But to give his acting a new dimension and the credit for his 'tragedy king' tag goes to Bimal Roy Productions' *Devdas*.

According to Anjum Rajabali, 'When you watch *Devdas*, you feel that Dilip Kumar was born to play that role. *Devdas* was written for Dilip Kumar to play his character, if I may say so myself...because the role fit him like a hand in glove. In his real life, Dilip Kumar was very different from the character— he had a towering personality with varied emotions. Yet he got so invested into the character of Devdas that it almost appeared to be the way he really is. It makes it very difficult to compare this to the same Dilip Kumar who was in *Ganga Jamuna*, in *Shakti*, in *Aan*, in *Andaz*, or in *Naya Daur*—that role defined the tragedy king in Dilip Kumar.'

Rajabali further explains that Dilip Kumar never made Devdas look weak. 'You don't think he's weak, you think of him as a lover. If there should be a lover, he should be like him—one who does not leave the conviction of his love.'

With the success of *Devdas*, the partnership between Bimal Roy Productions and Dilip Kumar was established, and this collaboration lead to the making of the studio's most successful film, a reincarnation drama—*Madhumati*.

Madhumati proved to be the biggest hit of 1958 and was honoured with nine Filmfare Awards. This record continued for thirty-seven years and was only broken in 1995 by *Dilwale Dulhania Le Jayenge* winning ten Filmfare Awards.

Filmmaker Vinay Shukla says, 'It is embedded in our psyche that reincarnations happen. We don't doubt that. The way Bimal Da presented reincarnation, it appeared so logical that nowhere do you feel that it is a fantasy. The high point of *Madhumati* is that you start believing in it. You start feeling that it is real.'

Today *Madhumati* may have cult status, but making it was no less than a miracle. Initially, Bimal Roy went to Nainital to shoot at a location more authentic to the script. But the heavy mist in the mountains destroyed the entire footage. Thus, the film had to be shot again and on sets created in Mumbai and Nasik. All this back and forth took the film's budget up to ₹1 crore, and every penny of the studio was at stake. Only after Bimal Roy had foregone his salary of ₹70 lakh, could the film release.

Amongst all the memorable aspects of *Madhumati*, the most special is its haunting music. For his biggest production, Bimal Roy chose Salil Chowdhury instead of S.D. Burman who had composed the music for his successful film, *Devdas*.

Salil Chowdhury had been associated with Bimal Roy for long, but he was going through a low phase in his career at that time and choosing him was a risk. Rinki Bhattacharya says, 'At that time, everybody was against Salil Choudhury and Shailendra. They would call them flop music directors. People suggested he hire Naushad or Shankar-Jaikishan instead. Back then, distributors would have a strong say in who was to be the music director for a film. But my father quietly went and signed Salil Choudhury.' For Salil Choudhury and Shailendra it was the biggest challenge because they knew that there was a lot of opposition to them becoming a part of *Madhumati*. After the film released, Salil Chowdhury made S.D. Burman listen to its entire album, who after listening to it said, 'Now if someone ever tells you that you are a flop music director, go back home. The industry doesn't deserve you.' After *Madhumati*, Salil Choudhury signed nineteen films.

The music and cinematography of *Madhumati* complement each other; a visual poetry is visible. And a big contribution to that is the fact that all its songs were choreographed by Bimal Roy himself.

Music director Shantanu Moitra says, 'If Bimal Roy is a

genius than Salil Chowdhury is also one. Salil Choudhury was present during the shooting of *Madhumati*. In the song "*Suhana Safar Aur Ye Mausam Hansi*" before the lyrics come there is a sound design, a bull is walking somewhere afar and its bells are lightly audible. This was originally not to be a part of the song. When the recording was going on, Salil Choudhury was there on Bimal Roy's insistence, they had heard it and included it in the song. It is amazing how foresighted they were. It's a practice in big Hollywood productions now, where they want the music composer also at the shoot just for continuity.'

In the video of that song you'll see that when Dilip Kumar walks, his feet are completely in sync with the beats of the song. They move with the beat and stop with it. He looks around and again starts with the song. This was all part of the choreography. And it was all done so gently that you don't even feel that it has been choreographed.

After the tremendous success of *Madhumati*, Bimal Roy Productions' next step amazed everybody. It proved that Bimal Roy was not a businessman but an artiste. In 1959, Bimal Roy turned towards his childhood memories where he had seen the exploitation of lower caste people. All these and more could be seen in the next film of the studio, *Sujata*.

Rinki Bhattacharya says that when she presented *Sujata* in a festival in Italy in an Indian festival, she was a little apprehensive thinking what would they know about the caste system in Italy? They don't know about caste or untouchability. When the screening ended, she realized how wrong she was because at the end of the film everybody came out crying. That is when she says she realized that it's not about the caste system. It was a much more fundamental fact; the bonding between the mother and the daughter, which doesn't take place because of this caste barrier. The triumph of the human spirit is so evident in this film that it is universal in nature.

For her nuanced performance in *Sujata*, Nutan got the Filmfare Award for Best Actress. Very few people know that before this film, Nutan was only seen in bold, glamorous and modern avatars in films. In the 1958 film *Dilli Ka Thug*, she had worn a swimsuit and shocked everybody. In that regard, by casting Nutan as a low-caste girl, Bimal Roy had once again showcased his brilliant casting instincts.

In the film's climax, Bimal Roy made a powerful statement about the difference of religion, caste, race and beauty being only superficial. And that we're all the same within.

Anjum Rajabali states, 'The last scene of the film is where Nutan, the Dalit girl, gives blood to Sunil Dutt's mother, who is a Brahmin, to save her life. This questioned that if a Brahmin could be saved by a Dalit's blood, what does it indicate? What is its implication? That a Dalit's blood can save a Brahmin. So don't look down on people belonging to lower castes, rather consider them your equal and be grateful to them and say, "Thank you very much. You are holding up our society." This is the best thing that comes out of the film, a social message which is being imparted.'

Bimal Roy won the Filmfare Award for the Best Director for *Sujata*. Up until then he had already won that award four times previously. People would even joke that he must retire otherwise no other director would get to win that award. But, Bimal Roy continued to make more brilliant films.

Between 1960 and 1962, three films were made in Bimal Roy Productions in which new directors were given a chance. Of these the landmark film was 1961's release, directed by Hemant Gupta and based on a short story by Tagore, *Kabuliwala*.

In 1969, came a film directed by Bimal Roy, which most people consider the masterpiece of his studio: *Bandini*—a love story which was adapted from Jarasandha's Bengali novel based on his experiences as a jailor.

Vinay Shukla says, 'Bimal Da was known to project the trends of the time on the screen in an organic and subtle manner, connecting it beautifully with his storytelling. *Bandini* left me completely spellbound. The utter simplicity of it, such minimalism; it was as if he had decided that he would keep this film as close to his heart as he can, the way he thinks, the way he sees things, he didn't compromise any aspect of the film.'

Narrated in flashbacks, Bandini is the story of Kalyani who is serving term in jail for a murder and finds herself in dilemma of choosing between the love of a revolutionary and a prison doctor. Although Nutan had already won the Filmfare Award for the Best Actress for *Sujata*, but many people believe *Bandini* to be the best performance of her career.

Bandini's music, which was inspired by the Bhatiyali folk Bengali music and classic raga Pilu, was composed by S.D. Burman. In the 50s and 60s, S.D. Burman was at the epitome of his range and success.

Music director Shantanu Moitra agrees and adds, 'Here was a man who could compose the entire soundtrack with just four instruments. He did not need the orchestra. It is an absolutely different school than of Salil Chowdhury. His melody was a song in itself. After signing up for *Bandini*, S.D. Burman did not take up any other work. For three months, he completely immersed himself into Bandini…he drowned himself in making the music which turned out to be some of his finest work.'

Another important feature of *Bandini* was that the then assistant director of Bimal Roy became a lyricist through this film. Today we know him as the Oscar winning lyricist, Gulzar.

Shantanu Moitra thanks Bimal Roy for giving us Gulzar. He says, otherwise Gulzar would have been a different person altogether. 'He was a mechanic who used to write poems as a hobby. Bimal Roy found him and took him straight to S.D. Burman and introduced him saying that he writes songs. S.D. Burman made him hear the tune of a keertan (a religious hymn). On that Gulzar wrote "*Mora Gora Rang Laile*".'

The climax of the film is counted amongst the best in Hindi cinema. The character of Kalyani, who was fighting the tussle between her past and future, capture and independence, had to choose between the characters of Devendra and Bikash.

Vinay Shukla adds that it was probably the first film where the resolution of the film comes from a song. 'Kalyani was going to meet Devendra, but then she sees Bikash on her way. Suddenly two paths open in front of her. She thinks that her dharma, her morals indicate that she should go with Bikash. But on the other side is life, there is a gratification of it, a happiness that she would get with Devendra. The lyrics of the title song—'*O Mere Majhi Mere Saajan Hain Uss Paar*'—portray her turmoil, her confusion and by the end of it her confusion gets cleared and she chooses to go back to Bikash.'

Bandini was awarded the National Award for Best Film in 1963. It also won six Filmfare Awards including for Best Film and Best Director. Bimal Roy Productions was at its peak at that time. But unfortunately *Bandini* was the last film of Bimal Roy. When he was working on his next film *Amrit Kumbh Ki Khoj Mein*, at the age of just fifty-six he died of cancer.

After Bimal Roy's death, the studio reduced to just a name. In 1968, after its last film of *Do Dooni Chaar*, the studio never made any film. But those who were trained at the studio kept the legacy of Bimal Roy alive in the days to come.

There is a trace of Bimal Roy's style of filmmaking in the films of Hrishikesh Mukherjee, Basu Chaterjee, Ritwik

Ghatak, Basu Bhattacharya and Gulzar.

Anjum Rajabali acknowledges, 'Hrishi Da was with Bimal Roy for a very long time; of course there was a cinematic influence on him, the gentleness in relationships and the honesty is visible in all of Hrishi Da's films, whether *Abhimaan* or other films like *Mili* and *Chupke Chupke*. Even in *Chupke Chupke* it was essentially a challenge to sustain a relationship of love with dignity and he presented it in a comic way. But Hrishikesh Mukherjee's films did not have that political overtones or undertones. So, his films remained in a personal sphere without necessarily touching upon a social issue in any prominent sort of way. That he did not do.'

Rinki Bhattacharya says that it was her father's dream, and he had said this in the piece which Gulzar wrote, that he wanted to be a part of our culture. He wanted to be remembered as someone who took the Indian culture forward. That is how she sees him. Bhattacharya calls him truly Indian and truly global.

More than all box office figures and awards, Bimal Roy Productions made cinema a medium of awakening society's consciousness. Erasing the dividing line between art and commerce, it made soulful, entertaining films and brought the Bengali literature and music into the mainstream. I believe that this is the biggest contribution of the studio in the Hindi film world and that is what makes Bimal Roy a truly immortal name.

FILMOGRAPHY

Do Bigha Zamin (1953)
Naukari (1954)
Devdas (1955)
Amaanat (1955)
Parivaar (1956)
Apradhi Kaun (1958)
Madhumati (1958)
Usne Kaha Tha (1960)
Sujata (1960)
Parakh (1960)
Kabuliwala (1961)
Prem Patra (1962)
Bandini (1963)
Benazir (1964)
Do Dooni Chaar (1968)

11

GURU DUTT FILMS PVT. LTD.

From Cinema to Classics

Founder: Guru Dutt (1925–64)

The studio owner made 8 memorable films in 10 years.

He achieved both commercial success and critical acclaim.

A National Award for Best Feature Film in Hindi.

Thirteen Filmfare Awards.

One silver jubilee and one golden jubilee.

The Studio's films showed an amazing game of light and shadow, criticism of the society, personal filmmaking and exhibition of idealism

In the era of studios, many studios played long and successful innings. R.K. Studios made twenty-one films in fifty-one years, Rajkamal Kalamandir made twenty-three films in forty-five years, Navketan made thirty-two films in five decades. Amidst these was another studio; one that made only eight films in total. But those films continue to be remembered for their personal themes, idealism and intricacies of human relationships, strong comments on society, and most importantly for evolution of cinema... film after film, year after year—Guru Dutt Films.

Behind the memorable movies by Guru Dutt Films, there was a visionary. It is interesting to note that the real name of that man was not even Guru Dutt.

The founder of the studio, Vasantkumar Shivshankar Padukone, was born on 9 July 1925 in Bangalore's Konkani Chitrapur in a Saraswat Brahmin family. Vasantkumar's childhood was spent near Kolkata in Bhawanipur. Bengali influence was so strong within and outside his house that Vasantkumar fashioned a new name for himself on the lines of Bengali names Dutt or Dutta, and kept it as Guru Dutt.

Between 1941 and 1944, he learned dance and music at Uday Shankar India Culture Centre, Almora. And in 1944 itself, at the age of nineteen he joined Prabhat Studios on a three-year contract as an assistant dance master.

At Prabhat Studios he met Dev Anand, the rising star of that time. Dev Anand was so impressed by Guru Dutt's personality and talent that he gave him a break as a director under his banner of Navketan Films in its second film *Baazi* (1951).

Baazi was a crime thriller. As an independent filmmaker, Guru Dutt made *Jaal* in 1952 with Dev Anand and *Baaz* in 1953 in which he acted for the first time.

In his initial films there is a distinct impression of noire—Hollywood crime thrillers of the 40s. Noire is a French word meaning black. It was a genre born in Hollywood in the 1930s, during the Great Depression.

Film historian Moinak Biswas says, 'Guru Dutt was probably the most sophisticated of all Indian filmmakers. His knowledge and grasp was very close to Hollywood. His films used to have everything: from vision being redirected to frames within frames; doorways, car windows, light, texture, street movement, the city and the city's look. Guru Dutt introduced it all beautifully.'

With the success of *Baazi*, *Jaal*, and *Baaz*, Guru Dutt got a firm grip on the industry and in 1954 decided to launch his own studio, which was called Guru Dutt Films Pvt. Ltd. The first film to be produced by it was *Aar-Paar* (1954)—it was in sync with his earlier directed noire films. From this film began the journey of Guru Dutt Films and Abrar Alvi, a collaboration which continued till *Sahib Bibi Aur Ghulam* in 1962.

According to film journalist and author Sathya Saran, 'Abrar was one of the first people to introduce natural language into Hindi cinema (where characters spoke the dialect of their own regions). Abrar said that he wanted to give different characters from different regions clear natural language. So, he gave dialogues for a Bombay guy to sound like a Bombay-walla, a Christian lady to talk like the way he thought they did. This was done for the first time, and it is like a textbook on dialogue writing. This is mimicked till today.'

Cinematographer V.K. Murthy worked for the first time with Guru Dutt in the film *Aar-Paar* and his brilliant cinematography made a place as an identity of Guru Dutt Films. Guru Dutt and V.K. Murthy shot most of the film *Aar-Paar* on the streets of Mumbai. For the first time a city got showcased as a character in the film.

Moinak Biswas elaborates on Dutt's approach, 'Post-Independence, Guru Dutt developed a style of portraying a city and modern life—for instance, how a man just loses himself in the crowd on a city's roads, someone who has moved to a city but gets so mesmerized by it that he doesn't miss the home he has left behind in his village, the vigour of a city like Mumbai and all that it gave him, a man trying to find his place in a new city—and his cameraman V.K. Murthy showing all of this in the films.'

'In *Aar-Par*, while V.K. Murthy gave birth to new ways of shooting and lighting, the new fashion in which the songs were picturized was invented by Guru Dutt. For instance, the songs in that film wouldn't begin with an introduction or a prelude, but with a dialogue,' explains Biswas.

The second film of the studio, *Mr & Mrs '55*, came in 1955 in which Guru Dutt was seen playing a cartoonist. What is interesting is that the cartoons used in the film were made by the famous cartoonist, the late R.K. Laxman himself. *Mr and Mrs '55* can be called a romantic comedy in today's time. It was through this film that Guru Dutt, for the first time, indicated his political leaning and taunted the society.

'You must have noticed that such people were well-versed with the political scenarios of that time. Guru Dutt used to touch upon such topics and raise prevalent issues which anyone without a keen sense of observation in politics could not have done. It was because of such awareness that he made a film like *Pyaasa* early in his career,' says Moinak Biswas.

Analysts believe that by 1956 Guru Dutt was bored of making formula films, he was growing more and more restless with the exploitative nature of man and society, artiste and business, ruler and the ruled...and the constant fights between them. One assumes that the artiste within Guru Dutt was struggling to express himself. With this desire, he started working on *Pyaasa*. But he was not just a director, he was also a studio owner—it was important to maintain a balance between art and commerce. Hence, along with directing *Pyaasa* he started work on *C.I.D.*

Sathya Saran gives us an insight when she says, '*C.I.D.* was purposefully made at the time so that just incase *Pyaasa* failed at the box office, there was an alternative to earn bread and butter from. He could not afford to suffer a huge loss because his unit would starve. He would starve. He was also married then. So, he had to keep his unit and himself afloat. It was a very conscious decision to simultaneously make one light, thriller film like *C.I.D,* which Dutt only produced and Raj Khosla directed, and a serious one like *Pyaasa*.'

Probably meant to be done on a lighter note, but in *C.I.D*, Guru Dutt Films' commentary on society got sharper. Music historian Rajiv Vijayakar tells us, 'Majrooh [Sultanpuri] Saheb was a Leftist, and very much against Nehru's politics because of which he was even jailed once. In the song "*Aye Dil Hai Mushkil Jeena Yahan*", he says things like that there are buildings, there are trams, etc.—you can get everything here except for a heart.[1] He probably got to write a song by a chance and he made complete use of the opportunity.'

Two debutants entered Hindi cinema through *C.I.D*. One was costume designer Bhanu Athaiya, who was later honoured with even an Oscar for the film *Gandhi*, in 1983. The other was the lead actress of the film itself, who was seen in every film made by the studio till *Saheb Bibi Aur Ghulam* in 1962: Waheeda Rehman—Guru Dutt's inspiration, his muse.

Sathya Saran tells us the story of how Waheeda Rehman was discovered, 'Somebody told Guru Dutt of a film called *Missamma* which was running in Hyderabad and doing very well, he suggested Dutt adapt it into a Hindi film. Together they watched the film but didn't like it much.

---

[1] Lyrics of the song are like this: Kahin building, *Kahin tramein (trams)/ Kahin motor, Kahin mill/Milta hai yahan sab kuch, Bas milta nahi dil/ Insaan ka nahin, Yahan naam-o-nishan.*

While discussing the film, they noticed a woman get out of a car and children in the street run after her as she entered the next building. Abrar was the first to ask what it was all about. He was told that she was a starlet who had acted in a Telugu film called *Rojulu Marayi*. Her dance in the film has made her extremely popular and the film extremely successful—it had been running in theatres for a hundred days. Dutt, Abrar and others watched that film, but were yet again left unimpressed. They drove off in their car and forgot all about Waheeda Rehman. Nobody ever thought that Waheeda Rehman would come into Hindi films. When they decided to adapt the American thriller film, *The Man with My Face,* into Hindi and call it *C.I.D*, they needed a dancer whose character had to seduce the hero.

In *Pyaasa* too they needed an actress to play the role of a dancer/sex worker, so they decided to call Waheeda Rehman.

Released in 1956, *C.I.D.* was a box office success. After three hit films, Guru Dutt Films was a successful studio and Guru Dutt himself was a successful producer. Had it been any other filmmaker, he would have continued making films of the same flavour...But in the conflict between art and commerce, the artiste in Guru Dutt was more powerful. Perhaps, more than delivering hit films, what he really wanted was to tell his point of view on things...to show a mirror to the society. All this and much more was seen in the next film by Guru Dutt Films, which was made in 1957 with an expenditure of ₹20 lakh—*Pyaasa*.

1957 was a turning point in Guru Dutt Films because from then began the studio's second and most famous era. It was the era when the studio's films not only produced cinematic brilliance but these films were also a slap on the so-called cultured society which snatches humanity from a human being. *Pyaasa* was the first film of this chain.

Film historian Ashish Rajadhyaksha says 'Guru Dutt created the idea of the existential angst in a man who will never belong to the absolute limit in films, like *Pyaasa* and *Kaagaz Ke Phool*. *Pyaasa* was inspired from a saying on the Greek poet Homer that reads, "Seven cities claimed Homer dead, while the living Homer begged his bread." The idea that the living poet will die in poverty, but the dead poet will be praised.'

In the film, Vijay was an unsuccessful poet, an outsider who gets thrown out of every strata of the society—a society which is high on riches, ego, selfishness and greed. The only solace he finds is in another outsider, a prostitute named Gulabo.

According to Sathya Saran, 'Guru Dutt had this idea of a socialite who would pick up young writers and painters, promote them, and then promptly drop them. The artistes would get emotionally involved but because she wanted to move on and make her name, she would drop them. This was Dutt's storyline. Abrar then told him his own story of his involvement with a Gulabo-like prostitute, how he knew her, how he used to visit her and they would chat all night.

How she would feed him when he was hungry; how he got busy with his films and neglected her and she later died of TB. He told the story to Guru Dutt, who said, "Bring her into our film. It will at least help you absolve yourself. It will be a cathartic release for you and it's a great story."'

Pyaasa got its ideological foundation from the famous Urdu poet, Sahir Ludhianvi, who took over from lyricist Majrooh Sultanpuri in Guru Dutt Films. Sahir's poetry was fearless and revolutionary, no less than a war cry.

Elaborating on Sahir Ludhianvi, Sathya Saran says, 'He always wrote about injustice. He was a flag bearer for justice. A poet with a sensitive nature like his was easily disappointed with many things in the newly Independent India back then. For Pyaasa, he wrote lyrics like—

Jinhe Naaz Hai Hind Par Who Kahan Hain?

(Where are those who felt extremely proud of Hindustan?)

Some people believe that these words of Sahir were a response to Pandit Nehru's speech, *Hume Hind Par Naaz Hai*, or maybe just sharp questions for him.

Film director Sudhir Mishra says, 'There was always a strong anti-capitalist stand in Sahir Ludhianvi's poetry. And Guru Dutt wasn't only anti-capitalist, but was against any oppressive system, anything that crushes the individuality of people, anything that does not accept the idea of different kind of people being able to coexist and anything that does not look after the most deprived. This is why he was against the idea of labelling someone as a sex worker or prostitute and then desolating her from the society. So, somewhere in the society, *Pyaasa*'s poet and prostitute were thrown into a similar situation in the society.'

Although the city is not mentioned in *Pyaasa* anywhere, but it is evident that the background for the story was Kolkata. The protagonist of the story was a poet—Bengal and especially Kolkata has always been the hub of art and literature. It is a possibility that that is why Guru Dutt chose Kolkata as the setting of the film.

With this film, another name joined the studio—composer-singer S.D. Burman who brought the touch of Bengali music into Guru Dutt Films. According to Rajiv Vijayakar, 'Guru Dutt had gradually come under the influence of Bengal as he made *Pyaasa*, *Kaagaz Ke Phool* or launched *Baharen Phir Bhi Aayengi* (which he could not complete himself). So, with their socialist angle, he must have felt that serious cinema needs a different kind of musician—one with a more Eastern influence. It was probably then that he found S.D. Burman suitable for the job.'

After *Mother India* and *Naya Daur*, *Pyaasa* was the third biggest hit of 1957. The irony was that the same society, which Guru Dutt had criticized in his film, watched it in thousands and lakhs, and made it a success. *Pyaasa*'s performance gave financial stability to the studio and the strength to further criticize the society, the foundation of which became Guru Dutt Films' next film, *Kaagaz Ke Phool*.

Released in 1959, *Kaagaz Ke Phool* had Guru Dutt raising questions about every system of the society—it's every structure. This was the most personal film to Guru Dutt. Narrated in flashback, *Kaagaz Ke Phool* is the story of a successful film director, Suresh Sinha, who is caught between his family and business.

Sathya Saran tells us, '*Kaagaz Ke Phool* was a theme which Guru Dutt had kept in his pocket since the time he was trying to become a director. He had that story with him since before *Aar-Par*. It was autobiographical in nature.'

Kaagaz Ke Phool was Hindi film industry's first CinemaScope film, which was made in collaboration with the Hollywood studio, 20th Century Fox. Though shooting the film in CinemaScope had increased the budget considerably, but aesthetically speaking the loneliness of the film's protagonists looked even thicker on 70 mm wide frames. Along with all that, the technical team played with light and shadow in picturizing the film's songs—a technique which is remembered even today.

Elaborating on the filming, Rajiv Vijayakar adds, 'Cinematographer V.K. Murthy's technical knowledge was tremendous. It was the era of black and white films, but Murthy was ahead of his time. He was even sent abroad for a short while, by Guru Dutt, to learn the latest technologies in filmmaking. Murthy was extremely talented, he would play with light and shadow to raise the emotions in the film and the mood being reflected in its songs.'

Sudhir Mishra says that Guru Dutt's songs were not mere redoing or shooting of the poem, 'They were an interpretation and the visual and the lyric and the music kind of created something else. It added and became something. It was not something that you have heard the song and that is sufficient. He was much-much more than anyone. The song, the lyric, the drama, the camera, the setting, the mood, the lighting all expresses something.'

In *Kaagaz Ke Phool*, Guru Dutt was critical of the society. The other filmmakers of his time, like Raj Kapoor, Bimal Roy, and others, would also criticize the society in their films. But Guru Dutt Films' style of social commentary was different from that of other studios.

According to Sathya Saran, 'Dutt's contemporary, Bimal Roy, also made similar films but they always had a message for the society, a very strong one. In Guru Dutt's films, however, you could not be sure whether there was a message or not. One tends to get so involved in the story that they forget to notice a subtle message. If the two are to be compared, it can be easily established that Guru Dutt was more of a poet and Bimal Roy a socialist.'

Film director Shyam Benegal compares the filmmaking of Raj Kapoor and that of Guru Dutt. He observes, 'Raj Kapoor was optimistic and in some ways also realistic. Guru Dutt was much more idealistic. Therefore, the sense of disappointment was even more obvious in the way he made his films. His films represented itself in very personal terms, whether you think of *Kaagaz Ke Phool*, *Pyaasa*, or any other. They can be seen as a personal prism. Their themes were not necessarily seen through a social prism, which Raj Kapoor did for his films.'

For Guru Dutt, *Kaagaz Ke Phool* was the result of his hard work of many years...it was his dream project. What could be a bigger irony than the fact that of all films he'd made the one that was closest to his heart went on to become a massive flop at the box office? Unintentionally, Guru Dutt ended up living the story of his film himself.

Sathya Saran informs us, 'The trouble with *Kaagaz Ke Phool* at the time was that people were just finding their feet in a new country—a newly liberated independent country. There was a whole new class of people in the economy that was rising: middle-class was just beginning to come up. They were very keen on matters like where will they find a house to live in, which city will they live in, what work can they find, will they find a job in this new country, they were low on hope because everything had been dismantled, shattered. Partition had displaced so many people. So the idea of 'roti (flatbread), kapda (clothes) aur makaan (house)' was very important, and what was this man making a film about? An esoteric film by Dutt, saying I am a creative man and I don't have creative satisfaction. People thought at least you have a job, you wear a suit and boot, you wear a hat, and you smoke a cigar... What is your problem in life? They rejected him.'

That flop is today counted amongst classics today. In

2002, the British film magazine, *Sight & Sound*, included *Kaagaz Ke Phool* in its list of 'The Greatest Films of All Time' based on a poll of 253 critics.

In 1959, after the failure of *Kaagaz Ke Phool* Guru Dutt Films was almost on the verge of shutting down. In such a situation, the studio began hiring directors from outside to make films for it in order to revive it. It was then that the studio thought it best to start afresh with a commercially viable love story. Thus, in 1960, Guru Dutt Films produced under Mohammed Sadiq's direction, *Chaudhvin Ka Chand*.

Chaudhvin Ka Chand is believed to be the most romantic movie of Guru Dutt Films. Although the film was in black and white, V.K. Murthy employed colour cinematography in the title song with the idea of adding a special hue to the colour of love.

According to Saran, 'Women went to see that film in droves because they hadn't seen such a man, in a long time, who stands and looks and talks about their beauty. It was not about grabbing your woman, slinging her on your shoulder and taking her into the cave. If you look at the romance shown in Raj Kapoor's films, you'll notice that though it was also very passionate but it has a North Indian sensibility there. It's very macho. Guru Dutt was a South Indian. Moreover, he was extremely influenced by the Bengali culture where women are revered and respected. His own mother was a role model for him.'

Chaudhvin Ka Chand was a hit at the box office. People

assumed that after a successful film, for the next one he will return to the director's chair. But at the last minute he handed over the baton to his friend and writer, Abrar Alvi. Subsequently, *Sahib Bibi Aur Ghulam* released in 1962, where another attempt was made to make a social comment.

Sathya Saran says, 'Guru Dutt had already tested Abrar's abilities in *Pyaasa*. One day, Abrar was told on *Pyaasa*'s set that Dutt had to go to court, when instead he was hiding upstairs, so he has to shoot the scene. Abrar did it and then noticed that the crew was looking up again and again. On looking up himself, he found Guru Dutt watching him from all the way there and looking happy. That was his test. Dutt had made up his mind then to launch Abrar Alvi as a director soon.'

By 1962, except for Sikkim, all other kingdoms had been integrated into the Independent India. Kings and kingly people were all the same now. Zamindar system was also abolished in the villages. *Sahib Bibi Aur Ghulam* was Guru Dutt Films' comment on these changing times, a changing country.

Moinak Biswas tells us that *Sahib Bibi Aur Ghulam* was an adaptation from Bimal Mitra's Bengali novel of the same name. 'However, the novel is nowhere near to the complex emotions shown in the film. With the kind of nuance and bravery, Guru Dutt had showcased the decline of the zamindari system, is a rare piece of art—hardly ever seen again in any film on social problems or political issues,' he adds.

The most memorable character of *Sahib Bibi Aur Ghulam* was 'Chhoti Bahu'. The character of Chhoti Bahu was played by Meena Kumari for which in 1963 she won the Filmfare Best Actress Award.

Sathya Saran says, 'Meena Kumari was a woman who had suffered herself like her character had. She was in a loveless marriage and was not treated very well by her husband—she brought all that to the fore in acting the character of Chhoti Bahu. She represented all those women who pined for their husband's attention. Everyone in the audience found a link of some kind, however minor or major.'

Sahib Bibi Aur Ghulam received four Filmfare Awards including the Best Picture. The film was also nominated for the Golden Bear at the Berlin International Film Festival.

Apart from all the praise, there was also a controversy attached to the film. Some people believe that it was not Abrar Alvi, but in fact Guru Dutt himself who had directed this film.

Saran elaborates it further, 'Abrar had said that he had learnt from the master by observing him. He knew nothing about cinema. He knew theatre and he was a writer, but nothing about film direction. He had learnt everything from Guru Dutt—from screenwriting to lighting, from cinematography to the placing of the camera and the placing of the rails, everything. So why wouldn't *Sahib Bibi Aur Ghulam* look like a Guru Dutt-directed film?'

Ernest Hemmingway had once said, 'Happiness in intelligent people is the rarest thing I know.' Guru Dutt too was a very zaheen (intelligent) man, and that is probably why he was not happy. With time, he engulfed himself in alcohol and two years after the release of *Sahib Bibi Aur Ghulam*—at the peak of his success—on 10 October 1964, Guru Dutt too committed suicide, like Hemmingway had.

Saran explains that Dutt had a manic depressive streak in him, which was accentuated by the alcohol and the fact that he took sleeping pills. Much after she wrote the book, *Ten Years with Guru Dutt: Abrar Alvi's Journey*, Saran says she was looking at soneryl tablets which Guru Dutt used to take and found that if you take soneryl tablets along with alcohol it leads to a deep depression.

When Guru Dutt committed suicide, he was only thirty-nine years old. Death at a young age often gives birth to many theories, stories and gossips. It makes a mythical figure of a human being. After the death of Guru Dutt, the second era of the evolution of Guru Dutt Films also ended.

Sudhir Mishra says, 'Guru Dutt was a very hard-working man. He used to be very careful with a film, its frames and the whole process of filmmaking. He wasn't just expressing his sadness or his agony but he was more than that. We must not ignore the metamorphosis of a man who had come from the commercial cinema genre into becoming an artiste with a sharp/critical eye. Very few people are like that today.'

Although Guru Dutt's younger brother, Atmaram, produced *Baharen Phir Bhi Aayengi*, *Shikar* and *Chanda Aur Bijli* under the banner of the studio, but the void left behind by Guru Dutt was impossible to fill. Gradually, the studio and its crew scattered. Compared to its contemporaries, Guru Dutt Films Pvt. Ltd. probably had the shortest duration in the industry.

'Guru Dutt made visuals, whether we term it as cinema or storytelling. He made visuals which remain in one's memory; he worked with themes which touched the heart; *Pyaasa* touches the heart, *Chaudhvin Ka Chand* touches the heart, tragedy and complex relationships that he brought forth, the balance of emotions that he portrayed, and the songs that he picturized so beautifully—they all remain. He created a brand of cinema which is unforgettable,' feels Sathya Saran.

Today, Guru Dutt is a source to learn from for all young filmmakers who want to make quality cinema. For me, it is not difficult to remember Guru Dutt, but to forget him is difficult. Whether it was music, new language of filmmaking, idealism, a different way of making a social comment, Guru Dutt is still an idol and inspiration for filmmakers. This is why the name of Guru Dutt Films is still alive as a *khwaabon ka safar*, and will always remain so.

FILMOGRAPHY

Baaz (1953)
Aar-Paar (1954)
Mr. & Mrs., '55 (1955)
C.I.D. (1956)
Pyaasa (1957)
Kaagaz Ke Phool (1959)
Chaudhvin Ka Chand (1960)
Sahib Biwi Aur Ghulam (1962)
Baharen Phir Bhi Ayengi (1966)
Shikar (1968)
Chanda Aur Bijli (1969)
Bindiya Chamkegi (1984)

12

B.R. FILMS

Meaningful Commercial Cinema

Founder: B.R. Chopra

Starting with a mere ₹2,000 the studio produced the first multi-starrer of Hindi cinema.

From the partition of the country to the partition of a home, B.R. Chopra made his studio the pillar of Hindi cinema.

The only studio to give a fight to the star system and radical fundamentalists.

Sixty years, thirty-four films, two National Awards, the Dadasaheb Phakle Award and Padma Bhushan.

In British India, Lahore was known as the cultural capital of India. When Partition took place, many artistes, like Balraj Sahni, Dev Anand, O.P. Nayyar, came to Mumbai. Amongst these stalwarts, another name surfaced, the USP of whose films were propagating social reforms, showing strong moral values and providing ace entertainment. The man, whose studio—B.R. Films—travelled through a journey of sixty years, from the black and white era to the television days of today, and which is still active—Baldev Raj Chopra, also called B.R. Chopra.

The founder of B.R. Films, B.R. Chopra, was born on 22 April 1914 in Ludhiana. He got his master's degree in English Literature from Government Law College, Lahore, where Chetan Anand and Balraj Sahni were his classmates. Since he always had an interest in films, after finishing college B.R. Chopra worked as a journalist for *Cine Herald* film magazine from 1944–47.

Senior film journalist I.M. Pannu says, 'His English was very good and he was well-versed with classic English literature. Most of his films were associated with society and its social issues and social limits. He presented prevalent scenarios in the form of stories and brought them on screen. So, the journalist within him could be seen at times in his films.'

In 1947, he stepped from film journalism into film production with the film *Chandni Chowk* but because of Partition the film had to be stopped. Like many other hundreds and thousands of people, Chopra family too lost everything they had in the riots. And B.R. Chopra with his wife Prakash, one-year-old-son, Ravi, and his young siblings—which included younger brother Yash Chopra—came to Mumbai.

B.R. Chopra lost everything that he had to Partition, but not his dream of making films. After struggling for three years, the financial condition of his house was still very weak. He had just ₹2,000 with him. But B.R. Chopra was a man of conviction and ambition.

Renu Chopra, daughter-in-law of B.R. Chopra, recalls, 'Persian Dairy at Churchgate used to be the hub of all film folks. He used to sit there without a clue what to do next. That day while leaving the house, his wife had told him that they were left with just ₹2,000. In Persian Dairy on that day he met I.S. Johar. They knew each other from Lahore, and on seeing him there, Johar went up to him and said, "Chopra, I have stories. Would you like to listen to them?" That's when he heard the story of *Afsana* and liked it a lot. He told Johar that he wants to buy this story from him but he has only ₹2,000 to spend. He told Johar that he would pay him the money after the film was made because that is all he had then. You can call it destiny, but on the table next to them was financier Govardhan Das, who had overheard the entire conversation and promised to back them.'

Since B.R. Chopra was a film journalist already he was aquainted with Ashok Kumar, whom he approached to play the lead in the film. Renu Chopra tells us, 'When Dada Muni [Ashok Kumar] heard the story, he immediately agreed to act in it but only on the condition that B.R. Chopra direct it himself. But he asked Dada Muni that how could he direct an entire film when he had never even held a camera in his hands. But Dada Muni was so convinced that he said to B.R. Chopra, "If you can reproduce on the silver screen even half of the narration you gave me, then this film will be a hit."'

Afsana released in 1951 and was a superhit, and with it B.R. Chopra became a film director in Mumbai.

Subsequently, he took the next big step of starting his own production house. As they say, behind every successful man there is a woman, the inspiration behind this step was his wife Prakash. She was the one to suggest B.R. Chopra to start B.R. Films.

Film journalist and author, Bharati Pradhan, says, 'His wife Prakash had a major role to play in making him a film producer. He had been making films for others but he became a film producer himself with the film *Ek Hi Rasta*. His wife used to ask him that how long he would make films for others. And that's why you would find the woman as tall as the man in their studio's logo. There is an old saying inscribed in it: *Ars Longa Vita Brevis* (Life may be short but creativity is immortal).'

In 1956, came the first film of the studio, *Ek Hi Rasta*, which B.R. Chopra directed himself. The film celebrated silver jubilee in theatres and was followed up, in 1957, with the film after the release of which B.R. Films came to be known as one of the most successful Hindi film studios.

Based on the theme of industrialization, this was the story of a coachman whose job and existence both get into jeopardy when bus service gets introduced in his village. It was the Dilip Kumar and Vyajanthimala starrer *Naya Daur*.

I.M. Pannu reflects that *Naya Daur* was based on the debate of man versus machine. 'It was a belief at that time that with the introduction of machines, men would be left with no jobs, but with *Naya Daur* B.R. Chopra told people that we can actually prosper with the association between man and machine. In those days, with the coming of motor vehicles or new mills or machines it was believed that men would be left without work. But B.R. Chopra tried to prove that perception wrong. He made that film in a way that it is just as relevant today for the debate of man versus computers.'

Naya Daur was 1957's second biggest hit, next to *Mother India*. An interesting fact is that the script of *Naya Daur* was termed non-commercial and refused by almost every studio of that time.

That subject had been going around in the industry but no one wanted to make a film on it. When B.R. Chopra decided to make *Naya Daur*, Mehboob Khan asked him why he wanted to make a 'documentary' on that subject. He tried to dissuade B.R. Chopra from doing so, but the latter had made up his mind and he made the film—a grand one at that.

After the film's premiere, Mehboob Khan confessed that he was wrong and Chopra was right and admitted that Chopra was a better filmmaker than he was, 'I could only imagine it as a documentary, but Chopra Sahab saw it as a feature film.'

By then the star system had its roots firmly in Hindi cinema, and those stars were kept at a high pedestal. Madhubala had originally signed up as the female lead for *Naya Daur*, but when she decided to drop out of it, then without getting bothered by the star system, B.R. Chopra took her to court.

Madhubala's father had barred her from stepping out of the house to shoot *Naya Daur* because he did not want any proximity between Dilip Kumar and his daughter. Challenged by this, B.R. Chopra decided to not have Madhubala in his film. He replaced her with Vyjayanthimala, but didn't forget to take Madhubala to court. This was the time when Dilip Kumar stood in court and declared that he loved Madhubala, cared for her, but what she did was unprofessional.

After the success of *Naya Daur*, the name B.R. Films was in the same league as R.K. Films, Navketan Studios and Guru Dutt Films. At this high point, B.R. Chopra decided to give a break to his younger brother, Yash Chopra, as a director who was until then assisting him in direction.

In 1959, B.R. Films produced *Dhool Ka Phool*: Yash Chopra's directorial debut. *Dhool Ka Phool* was the story of an illegitimate Hindu child who is brought up by a Muslim.

'There was so much Yash Chopra wanted to say about social justice and so he created the characters of a woman and an illegitimate child, which was way ahead of the times, much more than his brother,' says Bharati Pradhan.

With *Naya Daur* and *Dhool Ka Phool* it was evident that B.R. Films wasn't susceptible to market forces. B.R. Chopra only wanted to produce and direct the films which he believed in. In 1960, once again this same ideological stand of the studio was seen. When we think about it, the year in which musical blockbusters, like Shammi Kapoor's *Junglee* and Joy Mukherjee's *Love In Shimla*, were being made, B.R. Films made the first song-less film of Hindi cinema—*Kanoon*—a statement against capital punishment, a courtroom drama.

B.R. Chopra and Yash Chopra had witnessed the wounds of Partition. If in *Dhool Ka Phool* a comment was made on Hindu-Muslim relationship, then the gruesome face of Partition was ripped of naked in the 1961 film, *Dharmputra*. This was unacceptable to some Hindu extremist groups and even after the film winning the National Award, cinema halls were attacked.

Dharmputra was a film about Partition and the period after it when they had to flee from Lahore, Pakistan. At that time, a Muslim coachman had saved them and possibly that is why even after the terrors of Partition were over they both could not forget it.

'By now it was evident that B.R. Films through its every film wanted to comment on the society. The same could be seen in their 1963 film, *Gumrah*, starring Sunil Dutt, Ashok Kumar and Mala Sinha—where the pain of a married woman could be seen on being torn between the love of her husband and her lover,' says Bharati Pradhan.

'The climax of *Gumrah* shows the husband saying to his wife that her lover is standing at the door and that she has to make the decision right then—whether to be with her husband or go with the lover. She goes down, opens the door, and her lover takes her name, "Meena", to which she replies, "No, only Mrs Ashok lives here." And she shuts the door in his face. For me, this is drama and it was something that he [B.R. Chopra] believed in. He believed in women's choices. He came from a background where his mother and wife had very strong influence on him,' says Renu Chopra.

With *Gumrah*, the association of B.R. Films with music director Ravi began, which continued till *Nikaah* which came in 1982. Many songs of B.R. Films were memorable but it would not be wrong to say that the emphasis in B.R. Films was more on story and content than music.

Music historian Rajiv Vijayakar says, '*Gumrah*, *Humraz*, *Nikaah*: when we look back today, these films are considered musical films. Why? Because music was an important part of it, it was at that level and no song in these films was made solely with the purpose of it becoming popular or to sell records or to run the film. The primary intent of the songs was to get associated with the story, to lift the story and to take it forward.'

B.R. Chopra had directed the last two films of B.R. Films himself, but the most ambitious film of the studio—the story of separation and then union of three brothers, and India's first multi-starrer film—he gave the command of which to his younger brother, Yash Chopra.

With Raj Kumar, Sunil Dutt, Shashi Kapoor, Sadhana, Balraj Sahni, Sharmila Tagore and Rehman, in 1965, came *Waqt*. In it for the first time a larger than life, aspirational way of storytelling came to be seen. Swanky cars, opulent bungalows, wall-to-wall carpeting, chiffon sarees, all these later went on to become the trademark of Yash Chopra.

I.M. Pannu says, 'When B.R. Chopra prepared the story of *Waqt*, he had the Kapoor family in mind and wanted to caste them in the film; Prithviraj Kapoor and his three sons, Raj Kapoor, Shammi Kapoor and Shashi Kapoor. But a big producer suggested him that he should not make a film with a single family. People would not like to see them because they would watch the film as watching a family and not with the lost and found aspect. Chopra Sahab agreed to it and took Balraj Sahni, Sunil Dutt, Shashi Kapoor and Raj Kumar to make this film. Waqt was the first multi-starrer film of its time. It was a film with grandeur, music, the formula of lost and found—it became an iconic film in itself.'

Waqt became the biggest hit of 1965. Yash Chopra got the Filmfare Award for Best Director. B.R. Films had become one of the most successful studios in Mumbai. People began expecting equally grand films from the studio, but B.R. Films maintained its focus on new content and experimentation. After the biggest multi-starrer of Hindi cinema, in 1969 the studio made the second song-less film of Hindi cinema and with just two protagonists—*Ittefaq*, a remake of the British film *Signpost to Murder*.

I.M. Pannu says, 'It would not be wrong to say that *Ittefaq* (which means coincidence) was itself made by coincidence, because B.R. Chopra was making *Aadmi Aur Insaan* and its climax was yet to be shot when they got to know that the heroine of the film, Saira Banu, had left for America for four months. Now the question was what would he do during these four months? At that point, he had the script of *Ittefaq*. Neither did the film have a big budget nor did it require to be shot in outdoor locations, it could be made in a limited time.

'*Ittefaq* can also be called an experimental film because many new things were tried in the film and when it released, the experiments were all proven correct.'

In the beginning of the 70s, B.R. Films had two prime directors—elder brother B.R. Chopra and younger brother Yash. In 1970, inspired by Thomas Hardy's novel, *The Mayor of Casterbridge*, both the brothers started developing *Daag*. But as luck would have it, *Daag* was made not under B.R. Films, but under the banner of Yash Raj Films. Yash Chopra had decided to separate from his brother's studio and establish his own.

Bharati Pradhan tells us that B.R. Chopra was devastated by Yash Chopra leaving B.R. Films. 'He was heartbroken. He could never imagine life without Yash Chopra. For him Yash Chopra was not his brother but his eldest son and Ravi the second one, and it reflected in a very short clip in

Dastaan, which was a remake of his first film *Afsana.* His heart was not in his work because he was saddened by the separation and it was obvious from *Dastaan* because there were a lot of things which went wrong in it.'

Renu Chopra says, 'They parted very amicably because both had worked together on the story of *Daag* and while separating Yash Chopra had asked for B.R. Chopra's permission to make *Daag* as his first film. His elder brother always remained his mentor.'

In 1973, Yash Chopra, as the director for B.R. Films, was replaced by B.R. Chopra's son Ravi Chopra. In 1975, came *Zameer* made under Ravi Chopra's direction. Along with *Sholay* and *Deewar, Zameer* became the third biggest hit of Amitabh Bachchan in 1975.

If there's one decade in Hindi cinema which is considered interesting and colourful, it is the 70s. It was then that cinema was clearly divided into commercial films and art films. Between those two were directors like Hrishikesh Mukherjee and Basu Chatterjee who were although in the mainstream, but tried to make realistic, light-hearted films representing the middle-class. B.R. Films was known for its experimentation. Once again, they did a new experiment and chose to have Basu Chatterjee direct a film for the studio—*Chhoti Si Baat* (1976), and in the same genre two years later B.R. Chopra himself directed *Pati, Patni Aur Woh.*

Bharati Pradhan says, 'B.R. Chopra and his wife were holidaying in Japan. They were watching television when they saw the news of a married man having an affair with someone in his office and they thought it would make an interesting plot. After returning home, B.R. Chopra seriously thought about the subject and declared that he will make a film on it, but it would be a comedy. To that Prakash ji said, "For that you will have to take Basu Chatterjee because I have never seen you even smile on a joke." She was convinced that he didn't have a sense of humour, while he was sure that he would direct it himself.'

It is possible that Ravi Chopra wanted to carve an identity for himself, different from his father B.R. Chopra. It is probably why he introduced Hollywood's disaster films genre in Hindi cinema. Instead of the studio's regular music director, Ravi, he brought the young R.D. Burman and in 1980 made the most ambitious film of the studio—*The Burning Train*. That film was a multi-starrer with actors like Dharmendra, Vinod Khanna, Parveen Babi, Hema Malini and Neetu Singh. Stunts and special effects in Hindi cinema were never seen on such a large scale on the screen.

Bharati Pradhan says 'B.R. Chopra believed very strongly that the story is the king, but Ravi believed more in the technique while making *The Burning Train*. But it is things like these which make us feel the difference between the thought-process of two generations. Against big expectations, *The Burning Train* did not do well commercially. On the other hand, even at the age of 68 B.R. Chopra was not ready to retire. He still wanted to show the mirror to the society through his films. Thus, the same year B.R. Films released *Insaf Ka Tarazu*.'

Inspired by the 1976 American film, *Lipstick*, in this film B.R. Chopra had commented on the legal system against the rape victims. According to actor Raj Babbar, 'B.R. Chopra had taken a risk with *Insaf Ka Tarazu*. The Censor Board was keen on banning the film. Justice Bhagwati was a friend of B.R. Chopra and after watching the film he offered to write a letter in favour of the film's release. A copy of that letter was probably submitted to the Censor Board as well, and it explained to them why it was important to release that film. The relevance of that subject can be seen even today as this country strengthened the rape laws after the Nirbhaya gang rape case (2012). B.R. Chopra made a film to make such a law in 1980 itself.'

The year was 1982. The contemporaries of B.R. Films—Navketan Films and Rajkamal Kalamandir—were facing their decline. But this was the time when with its next film B.R. Films surprised both the critics and audience; the most controversial film—*Nikaah*.

It was the story of Niloufer who is divorced by her husband when he says 'Talaq' (divorce) to her thrice in a fit of anger. *Nikaah* raised questions about the Sharia laws for marriage and divorce. If *Dharmputra* had upset Hindu extremists, this time the Muslim hardliners were vehemently opposing a film.

Bharati Pradhan informs that a big group of Maulvis were against the film, 'The film also could not run for its first few days. But when B.R. Chopra showed the film to people and they realized that he was not commenting against any religion and was only trying to showcase a social issue, they let it release and it went on to become a superhit.'

For the protagonist of the film *Nikaah*, Niloufer, B.R. Chopra casted an unconventional face—Salma Agha, who had actually come to Mumbai from Pakistan to become a singer.

The screenwriter of *Nikaah*, Dr Achala Nagar shares an interesting anecdote, 'Salma had come to Mumbai to become a playback singer. She got to know that film's singer was Asha Bhonsle, she did not say anything but started to cry. When I got to know I told my father (Hindi writer and playwright Amritlal Nagar). He asked Ravi to make her the playback singer but Ravi felt it would be very difficult, "Her voice is like Shamshad Begum. How will we do it?" But my father said, "I don't know. I cannot break the girl's heart. Whatever it takes, you just make the change." Thus, Salma Agha got to do playback for herself in the film.'

Nikaah not only became a superhit film but Salma Agha also got the Filmfare Award for the Best Female Playback Singer. B.R. Films was continuously making meaningful commercial films in the 80s, but the studio was also about to turn towards a new medium.

In the 80s, along with cinema, television had also come up as a major source of entertainment. Especially, after the introduction of colour television in 1982, its popularity was getting ground with every passing year. B.R. Films recognized the power of television at the right time and in 1988 made the magnum opus *Mahabharat* for Doordarshan.

Bharati Pradhan says, 'Every time a film of his was to be released, he would get anxious and call the film a flop. He felt something similar for *Mahabharat* too because he had a few issues with the first episode where a few things, like a man is made from his actions, not the origin of birth,' were said. The Rajiv Gandhi government had even opposed it. It took a while for the first episode to be reinstated otherwise they would have had to move ahead without it.'

Mahabharat, comprising ninety-four episodes, was made with an investment of ₹9 crore. This weekly serial continued for two years and its appeal was such that even the streets would be empty at 9 o'clock every Sunday morning. Here too the amazing conviction of B.R. Films could be seen—to write screenplay for the biggest epic of the Hindus they chose a Muslim writer—Dr Rahi Masoom Raza.

Renu Chopra says, 'Armed with the pilot episode of *Mahabharat*, Ravi Chopra and Rahi Sahab went with B.R. Chopra to the Doordarshan office to submit it. However, without even looking at it, Mr Gill, the then Doordarshan head, said that it won't work because it had been written by a Muslim. B.R. Chopra asked him to see the pilot episode first and said that they could discuss things after that. *Mahabharat* begins with Time telling the epic—'*Main Samay Hoon...*'—which was an idea entirely conceived by Dr Raza. B.R. Chopra had so much faith in him that he declared in Doordarshan that if they wanted him to make *Mahabharat*, he would only do it with Rahi Masoom Raza or he would quit otherwise.'

B.R. Films stayed away from making films for the most of 90s. Although in 1991, Ravi Chopra made *Pratigyabadh* with Mithun Chakraborty and Kumar Gaurav; and in 1992, *Kal Ki Awaz* with Dharmendra and Raj Babbar—but both the films bombed at the box office. In 1998, B.R. Chopra was honoured with Dadasaheb Phalke Award for his Outstanding Contribution to Hindi cinema.

But it had been two decades since B.R. Films had given its last hit. Some people had begun to believe that the film journey of B.R. Films was over. In 2003, it was the age of modern love stories. In the time of Shahrukh Khan, Aamir Khan and Salman Khan, B.R. Films was making family drama with traditional values. Then the studio made a film on the story which B.R. Chopra had written himself decades ago—*Baghban*. Although *Baghban* was directed by Ravi Chopra but the vision behind the film was B.R. Chopra's.

Dr Achala Nagar recounts an interesting anecdote related to it. 'After B.R. Chopra watched the whole film, Ravi Chopra asked him how he liked the film. He asked, "What is the message going to the audience?" To which I tried to explain that the climax speech in it covered it all. But he was not convinced. He said, "All I am saying is that when the audience leaves the hall, what would they take back with them? Something is amiss." Then it struck us what he was trying to say and we added the part where the media asks Amitabh Bachchan's character that had this been the story of his family, what would have he done? To which the character replied that he would break his relationship with such children and walk away. The audience understood the message and even clapped in the end.'

With the magnanimous success of *Baghban* it was almost like the studio got a new lease of life. And three years later, on the golden jubilee of the studio, B.R. Films made *Baabul* starring Amitabh Bachchan, Salman Khan and Rani Mukerji on the theme of widow remarriage.

After producing thirty-four films, directing seventeen films, making the magnum opus *Mahabharat* for television and after being associated with Hindi cinema for six decades, on 5 November 2008, B.R. Chopra passed away. B.R. Chopra wasn't there anymore but his son Ravi Chopra kept B.R. Films alive and continued making films. But unfortunately on 12 November 2014 Ravi Chopra too passed away at the age of 68.

B.R. Films is still active in Mumbai. The third generation of Chopra family is ready to make films. The new generation may have a new thinking but they too want to maintain the ideology of B.R. Films.

Abhay Chopra, film director and grandson of B.R. Chopra, says, '*Bhoothnath* is the first film which my brother and I made independently. We even have a strong team of writers. In the last year, we have made stories for three films which we will soon start to work on.' He adds that he has to walk extra miles after his grandfather and that is the ideology which he carries about this studio. He believes they have a long way to go.

I.M. Pannu adds, 'B.R. Chopra's banner has given many memorable films. He made films that showed the mirror to the society. His films would not have a cabaret dance sequence or an action scene on distributors' demands. He made films purely on his own conviction, and which were appreciated too. His films were hits, they earned money and awards. He was a director who did complete justice to his stories.'

The journey from merely ₹2,000 to owning a film studio, separation of the brothers, the ups and downs of life and death—the story of B.R. Films itself is no less than any Bollywood saga. In its film journey of over sixty years, B.R. Films saw every colour of life and showed it on the silver screen too. A studio whose *khwaabon ka safar* continues even today.

FILMOGRAPHY

Afsana (1951)
Ek Hi Raasta (1956)
Naya Daur (1957)
Sadhna (1958)
Dhool Ka Phool (1959)
Kanoon (1961)
Dharmputra (1961)
Gumrah (1962)
Waqt (1965)

Humraz (1967)
Ittefaq (1969)
Aadmi Aur Insaan (1970)
Dastaan (1972)
Dhund (1973)
Zameer (1975)
Chhoti Si Baat (1975)
Karm (1977)
Pati Patni Aur Woh (1978)
The Burning Train (1980)
Insaf Ka Tarazoo (1980)
Agni Pareeksha (1981)
Nikaah (1982)
Mazdoor (1983)
Aaj Ki Awaaz (1984)
Kirayaddar (1986)
Dahleez (1986)
Awam (1987)
Pratigyabadh (1991)
Kal Ki Awaz (1992)
Mahabharat (1988 TV series)
Baghban (2003)
Baabul (2006)
Bhootnath (2008)
Heaven on Earth (2009)
Bhootnath Returns (2014)

13

FILMALAYA STUDIO

House of Romantic Comedies

Founder: Shashadhar Mukerji

Located in Mumbai, Andheri.

The studio made seven films in seven years.

Films were mostly romantic comedies shot in outdoor locations for the first time in Hindi cinema.

New fashion icons were born.

The last producer-owned filmmaking studio of the studio era.

Every story has three parts—beginning, interval and end. Like his films Shashadhar Mukerji's story also had three parts: his career in films started with Bombay Talkies, then he built Filmistan which was the interval of his story, and finally in 1958 began the third part of his life when he joined a new story with the journey of his dreams—Filmalaya.

Shubir Mukerji, filmmaker and son of Shashadhar Mukerji, says, 'The last film my father made for Filmistan was *Tumsa Nahi Dekha*. Then Filmalaya was created and it operated from our house Groto Villa in Santacruz, Mumbai. Rehearsals regularly took place in our house, with Nasir [Hussain] uncle and O.P. Nayyar being regulars there too.'

Filmalaya's speed was not as fast as Filmistan's. Here, only seven films were made in seven years but even in this short duration Filmalaya left its impact on Hindi cinema. Filmalaya gave Hindi cinema new fashion icons and made stars out of new talents. History has a tendency to repeat itself. Shashadhar Mukerji had started Filmistan with the team of the hit Bombay Talkies' film, *Kismet*; and then in 1958, he established Filmalaya with the team of the last Filmistan hit—*Tumsa Nahi Dekha*.

A new star had born out of *Tumsa Nahi Dekha*—Shammi Kapoor. The three big stars of that time: Dilip Kumar, Raj Kapoor and Dev Anand had been in the film industry for over fifteen years. But the very first film of Filmalaya, *Dil Deke Dekho*, stamped Shammi Kapoor as the new star of Hindi cinema.

Tanishaa Mukerji, actress and granddaughter of S. Mukherji, still remembers the title song of *Dil Deke Dekho*, 'I still love that song. The way Shammi Kapoor would have his shirt unbuttoned and the looks that he would give, even as kids we used to be in awe of him thinking that this person is amazing and what a style he had!'

Film journalist Ajay Brahmatmaj says, 'Shammi Kapoor had the image of a naughty hero, one who had no qualms about flirting with girls. His character would play pranks, tease the heroine, but deep down was always a good man. He would just do all that to get his lady love. All of this was happening for the first time in Hindi cinema. Before this, Bollywood films would end at the point where the hero touched the heroine's hand—and then came this drastic change where in the opening scene itself the hero could be seen teasing a girl.'

Dil Deke Dekho, *Munimji* and *Paying Guest* were along the same line as *Tumsa Nahi Dekha*. The outline of the storyline was the same as seen in the earlier films of Nasir Hussain: naughty hero, light comedy, gentle tiffs and then expression of love, which later went on to become the trademark style of Nasir Hussain.

According to Ajay Brahmatmaj, 'Nasir Hussain's films used to be musical and he added another aspect to it, which later on was adapted by others too—family members getting separated, and reuniting later. So Nasir Hussain created all these formulas and by giving successful films one after the other he asserted that his formulas produced guaranteed hits.'

Dil Deke Dekho introduced into the industry two new actors. Asha Parekh's debut in the film was magnanimous. And with this film, actor Prem Nath's younger brother

Rajendra Nath entered Hindi films as comedian.

Shubir Mukerji tells us, 'Asha Parekh had danced in a Durga Puja celebration, and my father had noticed her. In Dil Deke Dekho, there was to be a dance competition sequence for which he needed a heroine who was a great dancer because she would be competing with Shammi Kapoor. That's how Asha Parekh came into the picture and she danced beautifully.'

Trends were changing with the times and the film's take on it was shown through Neeta's character in the film. Though she had studied abroad, Neeta was a character which was modern yet had traditional Indian values—she would wear a saree and would dance to Western tunes too.

Tanishaa Mukerji explains, 'In *Dil Deke Dekho*, for the first time a heroine dressed in Indian attire was seen dancing to Western tunes. Earlier only the vamps were shown dancing to Western music. That film was path-breaking in the sense that it showed a perfect mix of the two cultures.'

Music has always been the high point of Shashadhar Mukerji's films. Finding new music composers and giving them an opportunity—this practice was started by Shashadhar Mukerji in Bombay Talkies itself. In Filmalaya, he gave a break to Usha Khanna in the very first film of the studio.

Music historian Rajiv Vijayakar says, 'It is amazing... if we trace S. Mukerji's work from Bombay Talkies to Filmalaya. These two banners gave Hindi cinema two female singers who became very famous—Saraswati Devi first, and then Usha Khanna in Nasir Hussain's directorial *Dil Deke Dekho* and two more films later, *Hum Hindustani* and *Aao Pyaar Karein*.'

Tanishaa Mukerji says, 'Elvis Presley was a major craze in the West during those years. It definitely had an impact on our film industry too because all our music makers used to dance to Elivis' songs too. So they created music along the same lines and made the Indian audience dance to that music too.'

In sync with the changing times, the film industry was also getting faster. People who could make successful films were not short of opportunities. After *Dil Deke Dekho*'s success Nasir Hussain also got busy trying to make films under his own banner, Nasir Hussain Films, and Shammi Kapoor too got pretty busy.

Shashadhar Mukerji then needed another hero for his next film for Filmalaya whom he found in his own home—Joy Mukherjee. There is always a story behind every new start in films. When Shashadhar Mukerji was looking for a new hero, he thought of his son, Joy. He was seen first as a hero in *Love In Shimla*. If Shammi Kapoor had adopted the style of Elvis Presley, then on the other hand Joy Mukherjee was known as the Rock Hudson of India. Avatar was the same, a naughty, chirpy hero.

Joy Mukherjee's son Sujoy Mukherjee reveals, 'Shashadhar Mukerji was planning a film called *Hum Hindustani* to be directed by his brother Ram Mukerji, for which he was looking for someone to play the younger brother to Sunil Dutt's character. Joy Mukherjee was found perfect for the role. But due to a lot of reasons, the film got delayed. Meanwhile, Filmalaya made another film, *Love In Shimla*, and launched Joy Mukherjee in it as the hero.'

With *Love In Shimla*, Filmalaya introduced another actress to the film industry—Sadhana. Dev Anand was probably the first male style icon of Hindi cinema, but then came Sadhana, whose Audrey Hepburn inspired hairstyle became a rage for the girls of the time making her the first female style icon of Bollywood.

Ajay Brahmatmaj says, 'It is said that she had a very broad forehead which didn't look very appealing on-screen. So the stylists brought her hair down on her forehead a bit, in order to make the face look smaller. This hairstyle became so popular among girls that it began to be referred to as the "Sadhana Cut".'

Eventually when *Hum Hindustani* did finally release in 1960, Shashadhar Mukerji had sent out a message of patriotism through it to the audience.

Tanishaa Mukerji says, 'He was very invested in his country and instilled the same patriotic values in his children too. Even my father had always encouraged us to vote, he would say things like, "You have to look out for your country, you have to be there for it."'

Indian People's Theatre Association still had an influence over Indian cinema. *Hum Hindustani*'s plot revolved around the clash of the new generation with the traditional Indian feudalism. In such a context, IPTA poet Prem Dhawan's lyrics fit perfectly for the film's music.

Ajay Brahmatmaj elaborates more on IPTA, 'Many progressive people were associated with it. One of them was Prem Dhawan, and *Hum Hindustani* was his story. IPTA members like Balraj Sahni, Chetan Anand and Prem Dhawan were a bunch of intellectuals, who were very active politically through their art. They harboured the dream of an India where there were equal opportunities for everyone.'

Sanjeev Kumar who went on to become one of the finest actors of Hindi cinema was first seen in *Hum Hindustani* in a small role. Shashadhar Mukerji made his first three films in his new studio with for new actors—Joy Mukherjee, Asha Parekh, Sadhana and Sanjeev Kumar—the credit of which goes to Filmalaya acting school which he had built to promote new talent.

Tanishaa Mukerji says, 'Not only just introduce new people, but he was also the kind of producer who would always give correct advice to those newcomers. After launching them through his own films, he never left them to fend for themselves. He nurtured a relationship with them, where the actors felt comfortable to discuss their ideas or anything else with him. That was what made a good producer great.'

Shubir Mukerji says, 'My father brought the best acting teacher from London. His name was P.T. Shenoy. He trained Asha Parekh, Sadhana, Joy Mukherjee and Sanjeev Kumar, and later even Kajol when she had gone to Filmalaya for a proper training in acting. Mr Shenoy was extremely good at his work and he never even charged any money for it. He did it as a policy.'

Filmalaya and Shashadhar Mukerji were now walking on their new journey. In 1962, released the fourth film of the studio, *Ek Musafir Ek Hasina*. In this film, Filmalaya repeated the hit pair of Joy Mukherjee and Sadhana. The film did a business of ₹2.5 crore on the box office and became the biggest hit of 1962.

A new trend started in the films of that time. Filmmakers started making films targeting the city audience by shooting those films in scenic outdoor locations. Most of the films of Filmalaya had not yet been influenced by that new trend. Most part of the film *Ek Musafir Ek Hasina* was shot in Kashmir, India.

Film historian and writer Anil Zankar adds, 'Even earlier, films were shot at outdoor locations. Like *Madhumati*, which had several outdoor scenes shot in nature's lap. It was a time when the themes for films began to be chosen according to the kind of characters it had, like a character who was shown stepping out of a plane will obviously also be shown living in a big city in a big house of his own. There was a Raj Kapoor film called *Around The World* (1967), which showed people on a world tour and that was a huge attraction.'

Storylines were going through a transition too, and in sync with that Filmalaya also experimented with its storytelling style. While *Love In Shimla*'s heroine was inspired by Cinderella's character, its storyline of the hero losing his memory—which became the pet formula of the films of the 70s and 80s—was first seen in *Ek Musafir Ek Hasina*.

Ajay Brahmatmaj points out that there is a very interesting phenomenon of Hindi cinema in the way it developed the relationship between a hero and heroine, which was very different from the way it was actually in the society. Like either of the characters losing their memory by getting hurt and then that memory coming back by being hit in the exact same place. This was a pure filmi formula with absolutely no scientific base to it. But because one film with such a plot became a hit, other directors and producers too began to use it in their films.

The 1962 war between India and China is seen as the end of Nehruvian Socialism. There was a disharmony breeding against the political class in India. This disharmony could be seen in Filmalaya's next release, Dilip Kumar starrer—*Leader*, which came out in 1964.

Ram Mukerji, director and nephew of Shashadhar Mukerji, says, '*Leader* was made twenty years too early. That film's theme is relevant in all times, even today industrialists are always busy collecting money. The film's climax showed Dilip Kumar saying:

Aapke ye sone aur chandi ke mehal toot toot kar

girjayenge. Aap logon ne jo paise kamaye hain sab galat dhandhon se hain. Aur ek din aaega jab...

(These palaces of yours made of gold and silver will soon demolish. You have earned only through wrong means and a day will come when...)

So this was an already discussed theory that a lot of exploitation was happening in the country.'

Before this Ram Mukerji had made *Hum Hindustani* for Filmalaya which had idealism, but *Leader* raised questions about the then politicians and their relationship with criminals. For the first time a political backdrop was used for storytelling. Incidentally, the film released the same year as Pandit Nehru passed away.

The hope that could be seen in the earlier films of Shashadhar Mukerji for his country was left behind somewhere. There was a deep hopelessness in *Leader* about the country's present and future.

Ajay Brahmatmaj says, 'The nexus of political leaders with businessmen or with the corrupt people could be seen in the Indian society, or the way they were trying to maintain their power by indulging the criminal minds of the society was getting obvious. Such news was coming to the forefront. This was the first time it was shown on the silver screen. And somewhere the corruption in the system, revolt against the system, and questioning the system—all these things can be seen in *Leader*.'

But, *Leader* was a failure at the box office. The next film by Filmalaya, also released in 1964, *Aao Pyaar Karen*, which was directed by the director of *Love in Shimla*, R.K. Nayyar, also bombed at the box office. With the failure of these films the downfall of Filmalaya had begun.

After the failures of 1964, Shashadhar Mukerji handed over the responsibility of filmmaking to his sons. Joy Mukherjee was already a star. In 1965, Shashadhar Mukerji's elder son, Rono Mukherjee, made a film on Goa's independence wherein he introduced his younger brother, Deb Mukherjee. Even this film could not set the cash registers ringing and with it the golden period of Filmalaya ended. At this point, everyone in the family started making their own banners. Filmalaya was left alone.

Shubir Mukherjee says, 'My father had retired from films. After the success of *Dil Deke Dekho*, *Love In Shimla*, which made Joy a star, *Ek Musafir Ek Hasina*—he was not into making films anymore. He got more involved in his health. He probably thought that his sons would take care of things there on. Joy became an actor, then Ram became a director and made *Leader* and *Hum Hindustani*. His brother Rono became a director, Deb became an actor and Shomu became a producer. I being the youngest joined the business and that too I didn't work my father, but instead for Gulshan Rai and made my first film, *Teesri Ankh*.'

Every story which has a beginning, has an end too. Shashadhar Mukerji's start happened with Bombay Talkies and for almost thirty years he contributed significantly to Hindi cinema for which the Indian Government conferred him with Padmashree in 1967.

Born on 29 September 1909, Shashadhar Mukerji passed

away in 1990. The journey of Filmalaya has ended but the studio still stands at its place. Today the building of the studio is given on rent for the shooting of films and serials. Shashadhar Mukerji's second and third generations are making films even now and are once again trying to reach that pinnacle of success, which was once touched by him.

Tanishaa Mukerji thinks, 'Different producers will carry forward the dreams of my grandfather and probably their own dreams too because you cannot get a gone generation back. You can only enjoy their work and feel that whatever they did was amazing but whatever the new generation is going to do now, would be done by them in their way. For example, Ayan [Deb Mukherjee's son] is making his own films now which are fabulous and amazing. He is taking it to another level in his own way, Kajol is doing her own thing, and so is Rani. All that began from one man's vision.'

Samrat Mukerji, actor and grandson of Shashadhar Mukerji, informs us, 'Today Filmalaya has more stages than it had before and they are planning to build even more sets. We are getting into production in a bigger way. Expansion is happening on all fronts. What is commendable is that all the generations of the Mukerjis have carved their own place in the industry without the help of the family name. So they themselves are today somebody in their own right and all of them are coming together now to make Filmalaya even bigger. So, the future of Filmalaya is in the hands of the next generation and at least they have got their ideas in the right place where they want Filmalaya to be.'

With the end of Filmalaya, the studio system of Hindi cinema where everything required in making a film used to be under one roof—actors, directors, technicians, fixed salaries, etc.—also ended. Bengal's New Theatres, Pune's Prabhat Studios and Mumbai's Bombay Talkies had already shut down. The end of Filmalaya was the end of studio system in the true sense.

Ajay Brahmatmaj reveals, 'All the studios of that time, along with Filmalaya, were on a decline because as a system, as an institution the studio system was failing. It was failing mainly because it did not have as creative minds as it did before. With all the studios together, somewhere filmmakers were connected and people like Shashadhar Mukerji, who were very creative, were no longer there. And it is not necessary that a creative man will have a creative son too.'

Ram Mukherjee says, 'It then became a hero–heroine oriented industry. The one who had a big hero/heroine could make a film, others had no such power. The rates of films kept on rising, the prices of artistes too escalated, which was beyond any producer's capability.'

By the 70s, cinema had got a firm foothold in this country. The structure was erected based on which it had become a little easy to make films. The filmmakers of that era had the strength of functioning without a studio. Many individual banners were seen during this time. The journey of films continued but this was the period of individual producers.

But today, once again a glimpse of the studio system can be seen in the Indian film industry. Film production companies are giving a chance to aspiring actors and making stars out of them. By giving directors and actors a contract for three films they are associating with them for long durations. The studio system cannot return, but once again such spaces are coming up in the Indian cinema which can be called a home for films.

Ajay Brahmatmaj elaborates, 'Whether Eros is doing it as a corporate house, or Dharma doing it individually with the name of Karan Johar, or Excel which has Farhan Akhtar and Ritesh Sidhwani—all of them are running production houses.' He remarks that studios cannot come back in their original form, but they do exist today in a different way and more in sync with current times, which is what is necessary.

Dreams come to us as stories, as tales, but the magic of taking the journey of dreams with eyes open is called cinema. The ones who laid the foundation of the studio system in India, the proprietor of cinema studios—Himansu Rai, B.N. Sircar, V. Shantaram, Shashadhar Mukerji, Dev Anand, Raj Kapoor and Guru Dutt—are those travellers of this *khwaabon ka safar* who in their studios created new dreams for the hundreds and thousands of film lovers in this country which can be seen even today on every Friday when a new film releases.

FILMOGRAPHY

Dil Deke Dekho (1959)
Love in Simla (1960)
Hum Hindustani (1960)
Ek Musafir Ek Hasina (1962)
Leader (1964)
Aao Pyar Karen (1964)
Tu Hi Meri Zindagi (1965)